Lexx Housewives Forever Knight Tin Man
by
Jim Fenn

"You're a pauper."
"But I'm not even married."

- The Three Stooges

Being parodies of:
Forever Knight
Lexx
Desperate Housewives
The Machine
The Island
Tin Man

I COULDN'T SLEEP AT ALL LAST NIGHT (Forever Knight)

He was brought over in 1228. That was his cabin number. Then he became a cop. He refused to play by the rules. Like the rule against being a vampire. Hey, that's vampirism! The vamps were going to picket but, you know, all that sunlight.

He wanders around his big studio apartment, gathering wine bottles. No, he does not drink – vine, but they don't make blood bottles. He has a buddy, Dr. Natty Bumpy, the town coroner, who is fascinated by a dead guy that walks around. "Most of my clients just lie there," she says. She has big fun making up potions to try to humanize Nick. Nick At Night, he calls himself.

His partner eats raw garlic on the advice of his health conscious wife. Nick is repelled by his breath. But then, so is everyone else. Their first case, a crazy with a machine gun and a couple of hostages. Nick uses his vampire powers to rise up several floors to the window and catch the guy. That's convenient.

Nick is tempted by a nearby archaeologist. He craves a Dry Sherry. But he tears himself away and hits the bottle instead. Natty Bumpy comes in, "You'll never get better as long as you drink this stuff."
"I yam what I yam."
"Okay, Popeye. How about a can of spinach?"

"I'm looking for a special jade cup that may cure vampirism. Croissant, my master, ran off with the other. Doesn't want me to turn back. You've heard of humanists? Croissant is an anti humanist."

Nick goes vampire hunting. Someone is killing street kids. With teeth. I mean biting their necks. He finds Black Jeans, the old buddy of his from the old country. [I'm guessing Swaziland.] She runs on about the good old days in Paris, Texas.

Back in his Cadillac, plenty of trunk space for a vampire nap, he flips on the radio and guess who the hot new nighttime DJ is, Croissant. Calls himself 'The Night Crawler.' [Isn't that a worm? How about the Night Hawk? The Night Rider? The Night of the Living Dead? Almost anything is better than Night Crawler. 'He crawls through the night, being ignored by one and all. Except maybe a hungry vole.'] "This one is dedicated to you, Nick At Night." He plays an ancient air on his violin. This puts Nick into a flashback during which he almost crashes the car. 'No cinematic flashbacks while driving. It's the law.'

Nick pulls into the radio station, "Fill her up with high test. And clean the windshield will ya, it's covered with night crawlers."
"Hey mac, this ain't no gas station, it's a radio station."
"Right. Okay, how about tuning my radio, it's full of Night Crawler."
Then there's the Night Creeper himself, Croissant. He guides Nick to the local blood bank. Puts in his ATM card, "Anything for you? They have a very nice A negative here."
"No thanks."
"Why do you hang out with those humies? Rejoin us, Nick."
The archaeologist followed them. Croissant makes a snack of her. She drops the precious jade cup. It smashes on the blood bank floor. As poor Nick drags himself back through Chinatown, he spots a storefront full of identical jade cups. It's tourist trash. Right next to the shelf full of monkey's paws.

Furry Lease, the archaeologist, calls the dept. "Where is my Nick At Night?"
"You want to report a missing TV channel," asks the long suffering desk sergeant. 'I thought I'd heard it all,' he thinks.
"No, Nick At Night, your vampire cop. I mean the cop who only works at night." She thinks, 'Whew, I almost gave away the secret.'
"You mean Toothy? He's vanished again. Look in his car trunk."

So Nick is hiding in the trunk, his partner, Skunky, decides to borrow the car. Just hope he doesn't put his dry cleaning in the trunk. On a sunny afternoon. Somebody is killing type O blood donors. Looks like it's Dr. Mephistopheles of the blood bank. He nips out and cuts the brake lines on the car because Skunky is nosing around.

"Are your brakes sluggish? Do you donate blood? Come on down to Honest John's Blood and Brakes! Relax in our state of the art donation room while we spruce up those old brakes on your car. Free orange juice and cookies for all customers. We'll bleed you dry while we bleed those brake lines. Come in today!"

Uh oh, the car is wrecked up. Garage man says, 'We'll have to use a torch just to open the trunk." The trunk containing Nick At Night. Vampires are definitely not fireproof. Nick somehow gets out. Maybe he does that 'turn into fog and seep through a crack' trick.

The blood bank guy goes to Nick's place to kill some more donors. The young lady pokes a burning broom at him. "Hey lady, I'm not Frankenstein, ya know."
"Frankenstein was the man, not the monster."
"You're about to die and you're correcting me?"
Nick flies in to save her but his place is on fire. [Does this guy have a dramatic life, or what?] He wants to bite the bad guy. [Go ahead, take a bite out of crime.] Croissant pops in and drains the blood bank guy. [Cut out the middle man, eh?] Right in front of Dry Sherry. "Archaeological Digest will never believe this," she says. Nick is weak from lack of blood. "Take me," says Sherry.
"Gee, I don't know."
"I can archaeologize future societies as a vampire."
"No!" He sticks Croissant with a burning piece of wood.

Chapter 2 – Father Annoying

Young priest keeps bugging old priest, "But what if he confessed that he was going to kill his wife? Would you report that?"
"No. Now get off my back! Young whippersnapper."

Then we see Skunky looking very out of place in a night club. Dances with a skank. Uh oh, she put in the light green contact lenses of a vampire! His badge won't fend off fangs.

Detective Night questions Father Annoying, "Any interesting confessions lately?" [Who is that guy? OMG! It's Kai of 'Lexx.' He can't be a father. He's a Devein assassin, reanimated to protect His Devein Shadow, who is secretly one of the Insect People. I see that I will have to write about 'Lexx' after this.]

Skunky is about to get bit. Nick's buddy, Black Jeans, chases him out.

Nick goes to church! [Don't they have a sign on the door, 'Vampires Not Allowed, This Means You'?] To look for clues to some religious style murders. He hides in the confessional. Skunky comes in, "Father, I want to confess."
In a very broad brogue, Nick says, "Yes, what is it my son?"
"I went into this club. My partner usually makes me wait outside. Anyway you wouldn't believe the dames in there. There was this one, Alum, or Evil–"
"It was Alum."
"Yeah, I remember now–" He pulls open the door, revealing Nick At Night.
"And maybe it is you should be listening to yon partner from now on it be," he says in a garbled Irish style.

Chapter 3 – The Psycho Psychic

"I'm losing my mind. I keep seeing images of that detective biting people's necks, drinking their blood, and killing them! And in period costume of centuries ago!" So Nick has to tell her he's a vampire. Soon he starts wearing a pin, 'I'm a vampire, ask me how.'

Psych gets shot. [Wouldn't a psychic know enough to dodge?] Nick picks her up and flies to the hospital. She says, "I can see my house from here." [What is it with people and seeing their house from the air? Can't you just enjoy the ride? This is some cheap effect. He's in front of a star field. Their hair isn't even blowing. Come on, you can get a cheap window fan for 20 bucks! Open your dang wallet. That's ten Townies for you Canadians. You know, the two dollar coin? This is another Canadian/German production, like Lexx. Good, innovative stuff.]

The gimmick on this show is that every case reminds Nick At Night of something in his past. And brother, he has one huge past! There's a murder in Chinatown. Not only does he remember something, the exact same folks are in it. The old man was a tiny boy when Nick was there last. [It's Low Main, from 'Big Trouble in Little China.']

Chapter 4 – Nude Alert!

Deborah Duchene, who plays Black Jeans, is wearing one of those sheer vampire gowns with apparently nothing under it. Or should I say everything under it. [This is maybe the first or second episode of Season 2. The first season came to be almost a standard cop show after a while so I skipped ahead.]

Oh, and Nick is under arrest for murder. They search his place and find bottles of blood in his fridge. Serial for breakfast, anyone? I think <u>Croissant</u> is back. [Maybe he was called away to be on 'Lexx.'] Nick says, "I use the blood as a paint thickener. Surely you've hear of 'painting the town red.'" For proof, he has some paint by numbers numbers on the wall.

Looks like they're pulling one of those 'maybe he's just crazy and imagined it all' bits. [I guessed it, Croissant was only lightly toasted. It helps that I have seen these before.]

Chapter 5 – Oh, Rice

This book writer they call Emily W. Ice, a thinly veiled <u>Anne Rice</u>. She writes about vampires. Nick says to her, "You seem to know all about us. I mean them."
She says, "Give me a break, dude. I just write stuff those turkeys will pay for. Morons."
[Oops, I may be channeling myself. I haven't been myself lately. I've been beside myself. I looked over and said, "Yipes!"]
Somebody tries to kill Ann Corn. Nick takes her to his place. He gets Black Jeans to guard White On Rice. Jeans says, "Oh come on, Nick, I hate her."
"Just keep your fangs sheathed for a few hours. I'll owe you big time."
"Only for you, Nick At Night."

Black Jeans has a big yen to bite Emily "They're only a myth" Lice. "They're only a hit or miss myth, Miss," she lisps shyly. [Say that 3 times fast!]

Look out, vampire writer and vampire are kissing. It's like something out of her oozy books. One expects various fluids to seep out of the pages. Skunky imagines himself as one of the vampires in the book. He really hams it up.

Someone sends threatening letters. [Probably her long time secretary. Ain't it always the way? Sort of like, 'The butler did it.']

Uh oh, he's nibbling her neck. Rather serious when a vampire does it. [Oh, she was reading aloud to a crowd.] Yep, it's her creepy little secretary. He tries to throw An Rise off the roof and jump with her.

Nick rescues her. Later he says to Natty, "I haven't really changed. I wanted to bite her. "
"But you didn't. You're a good vamp, like Angel, or the later Spike."
"I guess."

Chapter 6 – The Hound of Toronto?

Inspector Lucky Charms flies over from Ireland Yard. "It's the wee folk. They've been taking steroids by the barrow full and tearing folks apart. 'Call me wee will ya?' they say.
"Is this April Fool's Day? The only mythical creatures we believe in are vampires."
"How dull for ye."

Black Jeans says it's Jack the Ripper. [I say we change it to Jack R. I. P. He didn't even eat his victims. What a slacker.]

Lowery hops out all right, taking the other officer's gun. Later Nick says, "I trusted her and she was a bad egg. Where's the nearest blood bank? I want to drown my sorrows. [Ya know, if you're trying to quit drinking blood, keeping several bottles of it in your fridge may not be the best idea.]

Charms borrows Natty's car and rams Jack the Ribber. [Hey, how about using your own Vauxhall Austin Mini for that?] But not before Jack kills Detective One Episode, who was nervous about going into field work. Moral: If you're nervous, you might be horribly killed, SO DON'T BE NERVOUS!

Chapter 7 – Buffy?

A young lady in a parking garage. She looks left and right. There are some shady looking characters around. Skunky and Nick. She runs to her car and peels out. Our vampire wrestles the car to the ground. In a thick Southern accent she says, "Ah didn't do it. Ah'm gist another Canuck, hey? I mean, eh?"

Croissant is back on WEIRD FM. Reminds me of that lady in 'The Warriors.' These camera folks love the image of lips by an old fashioned microphone.

The bad gal, Lowery Garfield the Cat, claims she was framed for all those murders she did. "It were ma evil twin. Lack on that there soap opera?"

Nick plays Furry Lease on the pianoforte. Of course, the Moonlight Sonata; vampires are only allowed to play music with a nighttime theme like 'A Little Night Music,' and 'After Midnight.'

Nick At is taking the prisoner somewhere in his Caddy with the top down. All she has to do is hop out and run. She says, "Ah reckon Ah kin beat y'all city folk in a foot race fur shore. Why once I outran a mountain lion. Had to. He were wantin' my chitlins fur his supper."

Lowery hops out all right, taking the other officer's gun. Nick says, "I trusted her and she was a bad egg. Where's the nearest blood bank? I want to drown my sorrows. [Helpful hint, if you're trying to quit drinking blood, you might not want to keep several bottles of it in your fridge.]

Chapter 8 – Life, Death, or Lithe

Guy drops dead for no reason. At the nearby brain research lab, a a lady says there's a place between life and death, "We call it lithe," she says, "with second part like the end of the word death. Not very good but we're brain scientists, not wordsmiths. We're flat lining. People come back changed. Disease free, spiritual, maybe even a monkey. We figure, kill the patient and hope for the best."

Nick went toward the light after Croissant bit him. He walks along in a sheer robe. [Is that manties I see under there?] Funny, the "good" lady wears a black robe. "It's just so slimming," she explains.

Nick says to Natty, "I've got to go back there. Go into the light. I simply must know about the white and black robe thing."
"It's dangerous."
"What's it going to do, kill me? I'm a vampire, remember?"
He goes near the light and has a nice chat with Dudley Death. "So, ya wanna go, or ya wanna stay," asks Death.
Nick flips a coin. Natty Bumpy rushes in and gives him some rat poison. [This you call a friend?] In the Desert of Death, Nick is saying, "Now was it heads go back, or tails stay dead?"
He revives. Bumpy says, "So, did you learn anything?"
"Yeah, always carry a two headed coin."

Chapter 9 – Ring Benefits

The M. E., or coroner, Natty Bumpy, slips a ring off a corpse's finger, weighs it in her hand, "18 karat, 50 bucks tops." She remembers someone else in in the room, "Ahem, I mean, I'll just put this in the evidence bag."

Bumpy comes up with another potion for Nick. "What is it?"
"Well, it was supposed to increase a bull's, um, ability, but it killed them."
"So what will it do to me?"
"Well, it will either cure you, or you may have a whole new career down on the farm."
He tries it. Goes out in the sun, "Look, I'm a sundial."
He and Bumpy go for a daylight ride with the top down. He goes to tell Black Jeans, "Take this and you could be White Jeans for a change. Make that Tan Jeans – khakis." He laughs. Nick is giddy. She says, "Don't try to change Jeans's jeans."

In the bright sunshine, Skunky says to Nick, "You look different. New haircut?"
"It's the sunshine. My allergy, I'm cured. New medicine."
They go to question a mob boss. Nick starts eating off his plate. He hasn't eaten in 800 years. The guy gives up and walks away, "Mangia."

Laid back Nick is hyper. Then he sees a woman. Has it been 800 years for that too? He fantasizes biting her neck, vampire style. Uh oh, he's vamping out. Rushes home and guzzles blood. He shoots up the bull stuff. Goes back to human, more or less. It's just a quick fix that doesn't last. He breaks into Bumpy's drug cabinet. Meets Mob Man, gets shot with bullets. Clean up guy puts him in the trunk of the Caddy. Take to lake, open trunk. Luckily the sun has gone down. Nick vamps out and puts the kibosh on the baddies.

Chapter 10 – Bye Bye World

A huge astronomer's tool discovers the end of the world. "Look, there it is, 'The End.' Printed on the North Pole. Oh wait, it says, 'This End Up.' Never mind. Okay, seriously; what would you do if a huge meteor hit the Earth? Bigger than the dinosaur killer of a while back? [I'd do the same things I do already.]

Skunky says, "God is going to wipe us out after all our progress?"
"What progress?"
"I don't know, fiber optics, air bags?"
Later they find that the giant meteor was only a speck on the lens.

THE END FOR NOW

BEZOAR AND BE FOXY (Zorro)

A traveling hypnotist [and aren't they annoying?] hypnotizes Don
Diego, not realizing he has also hypnotized Bezoar, the Fox! The Old
Coldly convicts Tim Reid on suspicion of being Venus Flytrap of
WKRP. "A crime made worse by the fact that radio has not even
been invented yet," he exclaims. Anyway, Bezoar goes around
robbing everyone.

Little Flipper ties him up. [He's the deaf dumb and blind kid that, in
between playing pinball, helps Bezoar around the cave. Funny thing,
in the original it was a man called Bernardino, Flipper was Friar
Tuck.]

Whenever anyone says, 'Eat two brunches,' Don Diego goes under or
snaps out of it. [You'd think that phrase would be uncommon, but
no.] Anyway, Bezoar somehow straightens things out while I went
for a cup of coffee.

THE END FOR NOW

EX (Lexx)

Chapter 1 – I Were Shipping Shadows

K, AKA the young priest in that 'Forever Knight' episode known as
the one where Ted Knight goes to church and Skunky confesses to
him, voices over, 'I am K, last of the Bruin Gee, who led humanity in
the last war against the insects." The one man ships look like
moths, attacking a mother ship shaped like a spider. [Okay bugs, we
get it.] He Shadowy wears a segmented hood that hides his face.
[Real trustworthy.] He kills K, who in later centuries was realized to
be the most special of the Bruin Gee. Thus he was honored with the
honorific, 'Special K.'

The screen says, '2008 years later.' [This show spans thousands of
years and takes place in two universes, and yet still manages to be
sleazy. That's my kind of show.] Screen says, 'The Cluster F**k,

[short for fire truck,] Capital of the League of 20,000 Planets Beneath the Sea.'

Our hero (?) is a slacker named Stain D. Wheedle Dumb. The "D" stands for nothing. The poor shlub added it to try to appear less average. He is a security guard class 4, needless to say, the lowest class. We see a majestic view of several rectangular space ships coming in to dock at a huge amphitheater in the sky. [Good effects for 1997, the olden days.] Beneath the majesty, Stain is tossing various objects at a bin to pass the tedious time. Someone asks for clearance to land. In the universal, nay multi universal, way of minor officials, he messes with her. A higher ranking person shows up and Stain is in big trouble.

A criminal is executed so as to receive He's Shadowy into another host body. It's a rush job so there may be complications. [Let's face it, there will be complications.] They pop out the old guy's brain and hook it up to the brain-o-matic brain preserver. The Devein Shadowy goes up on this automated Stonehenge thing. The old brains say, "The Ex is nearly ready to destroy planets, but which ones?"
New Guy says, "Heck, why not destroy them all? Got to break eggs to make omelets." He packs up the brains for shipment.

A line of prisoners shackled to moving walls, rolls forward, stops. Holographic images appear, they try and convict each prisoner automatically. They read this guy's brain. He refused to pay tithes. He becomes a total body donor, effective immediately. Sieve is selected to be transformed into a love slave. Next, the arch heretic, Throw Din, who will be executed in the amphitheater by being devoured by cluster lizards, a sort of rolling alligator. But he has a smart bomb up his nose. [Yes, that's what I said.] The bomb has to find a cable to destroy which will free Throw Din. The bug blows and the cluster lizards are released to devour a group of boy scouts. Throw Din escapes, Sieve is in the transformer. Stain is sentenced to termination. A cluster lizard enters the love slave room. Also, Jiggle Otter, who wears a suit of human skin, is freed by the great hero, Throw Din. The lizard attacks Sieve! The machine smashes it. She's transformed into a part woman/part cluster lizard. The machine prepares to program her brain. She pops a robot head in her place. The robot falls in love with her.

A pair of heavily armed robot guards prepare to blow Sieve, of Beefy Cake, away, for the crime of, whatever. She hides behind Stain. They run into a couple of lizards. Sieve shrieks at them. The lizards say, "Mommy," and eat the guards.

We see an image of the Ex, a spaceship shaped like a wasp with a long body. Make that a dragonfly. [Note to self, edit out wasp bit.] The crazy new Devein Shadowy wakens K, the Devein Assassin. With his Batarang, he can devein a shrimp at one hundred paces. At the door to the Ex, Throw Din passes off the key, which is a sort of electric virus which may be possessed by only one person at a time, kisses the girl, makes a manly speech, and faces K, and certain death. [What a dimwit.] A leftover lizard eats the other guy which releases the key to Stain D. Wheedle. Now Stain D. Wheedle, security guard 4th class, commands the most powerful—wait, that comes later.

Jiggle slips in with Stain into a Fly, a bred flying machine like a living helicopter. Sieve grabs the landing gear. Thrown turns invisible and cuts K's head and arm off. K shrugs, he wasn't much of a thinker anyway. K shoots his Batarang at Throw Din and pulls himself together.

Stain puts his hand on the floating hand image in the ship. A big voice says, "What planet do you want me to destroy?"
Stain says, "Take us out of here, Mr. Sulu."
The giant insect shrugs and takes off. And so begin the adventures of Sieve, Jiggle Otter, and Stain D. Wheedle.

The worm turns. On the way out, an officious little person demands the exit code. Stain says, "Oh Ex, could you blow up that planetoid over there?"
"Sure, boss." The giant bug sends out a wide beam which destroys the planetoid and the whole planet behind it. Then He's Devein Shadowy comes to attack and, somehow, K appears aboard the Ex. He throws Jiggle Otter off the bridge. [Okay, riddle me this. How do these spaceships have a big open hole without all the air rushing out? I've seen this on three different science fiction shows. I suppose it's dramatic, so to heck with making sense, right?] He's about to execute Stain and Sieve when the brains yell for help. A cluster lizard is eating them. K kills the lizard and then accidentally learns of his past as the last of the Bruin Gee and the enemy of He's Shadowy. He says, "Holy Gee, I'm playing for the wrong team!" He goes back to the Ex and does his famous speech, "I've killed mothers with their babies, great philosophers, proud young warriors, the good, the bad, the ugly . . . so, you guys hiring?"

He's Shadowy appears! K says he's going to off the brains. He jumps off the bridge. The Ex is heading for a black hole. He's Shadowy attacks K in the brain room. Stain and Sieve start smashing brains. He's Shadowy weakens. K Batarangs the top of He's head off. The Ex enters the singularity. Sieve gives the glad eye to K. They made it. But the enemy ship is still after them. The Ex is programmed not to fire at He's Shadowy ships. But the black hole changed that. They blow the baddies away.

The Robot Head says, "The stars here are uncharted."
They've crossed over, into the Twilight Zone. K takes a dirt nap. "My dodo blood is limited. Don't wake me except for new episodes of 'Big Bang Theory.'"

Chapter 2 – Super Duper Nova

[I don't remember any super nova. Oh wait, is this the one with that actor, you know the one, last guy on his planet which is about to be eaten up by a super nova?] We open with a voice over by the Ex, 'I am the most powerful weapon in two universes. I work for Stain D. Wheedle. Well, what you going to do? He has the key.' The big ship rambles on a while. It doesn't get out much. So to speak.

A sort of flying coffin appears in space. A message broadcasts, "My people have sent me into the depths of space searching for a cure for the plague which threaten our entire–" SPLAT! It crashes into the Ex, which doesn't even notice. [This ain't Star Trek, folks.] Sieve goes to the deep freeze to moon over her dead boyfriend. The robot head, 7.99 Plus Tax, endlessly recites love poetry about Sieve.

Stain wakes up and the three of them instantly start arguing. It's a love quadrangle. Stain wants Sieve, Sieve wants K, 7.99 wants Sieve, K claims to want nothing. At least they're rid of Jiggle Otter. Oops, she falls into a lake of dodo blood and reanimates.

Sieve showers. All plumbing is organically grown as part of the ship. Speaking of groan, Stain is watching her. He says, "Now come on Sieve, we're the only two people in this universe. You are a love slave."
She says, "Only my body. My sexual drive has increased beyond measure. I need to be caressed, stroked."
"Yes!"
"But not by you."

K has a cell phone tattooed to his face. So old fashioned. On the planet, Poetic Dude, Tim Curry, says, "I chose to stay behind when our race left this doomed planet. Okay, they chose to leave me behind. Claimed I never shut up. Well, I never."

They all "select" ways to die. It's a suicide parlor. Can K save them? Find out after these messages.

The guys chat with a couple of stars. Big balls of gas. Heavenly bodies. Suns. K wants to stay and die. Again. [Why am I writing like that fish guy? You know, 'The old man had been 87 days without a fish. He thought, 'Maybe if I baited the hooks?'] Sieve convinces K to come. They leave just as the super is novaing. Only Jiggle Otter is left behind. She's flash baked. 'If only I could eat myself,' is her last thought.

Chapter 3 – Giggle Shadow

[I skipped the third part, 'Eating Pattern.' Sort of a cannibal planet thing. The 1st season is four feature length films. After that is three seasons of hour long shows. The Caterpillar Woman has a huge monolog about the earlier shows. You might want to step out for coffee. Heck, step out and plant some coffee bean bushes. By the time she's done, the plants will grow up and produce fresh beans. I went back and timed it. Her thing, plus Ex's usual opening bit, adds up to 8 solid minutes before any action takes place. This is a show that breaks all the rules. The thing is, some rules are better left unbroken.]

Finally some action. Of a sort. Bunch of religious nuts standing around, chanting. If you're offended, these guys worship the essence of an insect, so there. Next thing they'll be sticking daggers into somebody. Malcolm MacDowell plays Yahtzee. He looks like the dagger type. I guessed it, they all put daggers to each other's throats. It's part of the ceremony. After so many coups they said, 'What the heck, make it part of the ceremony.' Big monk fight. Malcolm takes one in the neck. Dies. Not worth his time showing up.

Stain complains about the food produced by the living ship. Sieve says, "We need to go back to the Cluster for more dodo blood for K. [They keep going on about him running out but he lasts the whole series. Caution, previous sentence may contain a spoiler.]

We go back in time to when Stain D. Wheedle fell for a trick and was captured and his tooth read. The brains in jars laugh at him. [Pretty bad when bodiless brains have a better life than you.]

Aw, K finds a baby cluster lizard. So cute, it's trying to eat Daddy's ear. "I'll name him Squash, after my favorite sport and vegetable." K and Sieve do a mind reading act. K channels the Shadowy and lip synchs him saying, "The Giggle Shadowy is the end. And the beginning." [Sounds like the kind of thing you might want to put on a robe and stab somebody over.] K ends up throwing Sieve across the room. [That's religion for ya. I'm a casual Buddhist myself. A little meditating, a little nature loving. No robes, no stabbing. I mean I do have a robe. I put it on after bathing.]

Sieve says to Stain, "I don't want to live with out K. He's special to me."
"I know, you love your Special K." [If you don't know, Special K is a health cereal by Kellogg. Also a joke by Eddie Murphy. Buckwheat was a 'Little Rascal' and the one that's a little slow is called Special K.]

Of course they finally go through 'the fracas' to the light universe. Stain stays home and the others take a Fly to the dodo blood store. But it's Shadowy Day so most stores are closed. They stop at a mini mall. "There's got to be a convenience store open somewhere." They find Malcolm MacDowell. "Not long dead," says K. They hear the mellifluous tones of He's Shadowy. He's lost a lot of weight. He's nothing but a brain. He claims to be good now. "Kill it," says Sieve. "Oh all right. Kill kill kill, that's all I ever do. I've killed babies with their mothers in strollers, the old, the halt, the lame, the sick, the slightly under the weather, the 'just have the blahs,' those affected with a hangnail . . . "

Some dodo blood drops into Malcolm MacDowell's mouth and he reanimates. [What do you bet he's a bad guy?] That lying brain! It hid the Shadowy which gets into M. M., or Yahtzee, as he calls himself. "I'm a fun game, not an evil bug thing!" Yahtzee kills himself but it doesn't take. He's a Shadow puppet now.

K dies again. Killing or dying, this guy is not much for the in between stuff. When he has some spare time, he crawls into a freezer.

The Giggle Shadow is an enormous brain. Sieve scoops up some dodo blood which is an oozy whitish thick liquid.

Meanwhile, Stain has been caught by the same guys that caught him before when he was a courier.

Squash saves K. The Giggle Shadow says, "You're too late, K." The favorite food of cluster lizards is brains. K sics his pet on the giant brain of the Giggle Shadow. It will giggle no more. Or will it? It sends a tendril after them. Little Squash finds the big brain and digs in. The Giggle Shadow dies. K says, "That's my boy."

Chapter 4 – Man Treed

A part of the shadow survives and spreads to humans. Or is this a flashback? Also, the Shadow snuck into K at the end of the last episode. [Mostly it's like 'Red Dwarf,' the last few humans in a spaceship, scrounging around and running into mostly bad guys. The actress, Eva Habermann, is pretty, but cold. Soon they will switch to Xenia Seeberg, who instantly becomes a huge fan favorite.]

K is putting in the black contact lenses of insectoid evil. [I could never be an actor. Contact lenses are icky. Poor Nigel Bennett, who played Croissant in 'Forever Knight,' passed out when he first put in the vampire contacts. He stars later on this show as 'That Guy That Refuses To Wear Contacts.' But let's not get ahead of ourselves.] K insists they go back to the "light" universe because the dodo blood there has less calories.

They take some Flies out and bring a huge chunk of bug aboard. K is bugging. Then they find some weird guys. Man Treed has unattached robot arms. The bug kills Man Treed and sucks the essence out of K. Like Bender of 'Futurama,' Man Treed's new motto is, 'Kill all humans.' Ex destroys the planet. They fly away. Followed by a few robot arms.

Chapter 5 – Sieve in a Bucket

[I mentioned the gals, the guys are Brian Downey as Stain D. Wheedle, and Michael McManus as Special K, and Jeffrey Hirschfield as the voice of 7.99.]

Stain and 7.99 serenade Sieve. She covers her ears. She wakes up K. Rather, Stain unfreezes him in a sloppy way, and K kills him while half asleep. "If I don't get at least a month's sleep, I'm grouchy all day," he says. They freeze Stain and Sieve gets the key with a kiss.

They find a floating hospital. [Is that like a floating crap game?] This is where Sieve is transformed into Rev, who revs up libidos. Or does she?

They fix up Stain and the doctor hits on Sieve. He says, "Drop those losers and you and me will fly the friendly skies in the Ex." She says no and he slips her a mickey. Dr. Bozo and Dr. Baldy want the Ex key. She changes into a cluster lizard and rolls away. And eats evil Dr. Baldy.

7.99 hijacks Stain's hospital bed. Bozo and Dr. Brylcreem try to kill K with radiation. Sieve pushes him out of harm's way and is turned into glop. 7.99 weeps. K dips up a bucket of Sieve.

Back on the ship they put her in a giant brandy snifter. The Man Treed arms eat the hospital.

Chapter 6 – So Where's the New Sieve?

A new woman appears. Not the new Sieve. She drops out of a plant. She is formed from Stain's dream. "Hi, I'm Licker," she says.

Nearby, some astronauts leave their atmosphere for the first time. Imagine running into the Ex and its crew first time out in space. They call their planet Cornfield because they're all simple farmers.

The astronauts come aboard the Ex. Luckily they speak English. "So what are you guys? We're humanoid."
"Well," says Stain, "I'm human, um, she's a plant, K was human 2009 years ago, 7.99 Plus Tax is a robot head in love with Sieve who is that bowl of glop over there." [If I was those astronauts, I'd be sidling toward the door about now.]

Stain shows off by saying, "Why, if I was to say, 'Ex, blow up that planet over there-'"
"As you wish, captain." Ex blows up the planet. Unfortunately, the space shuttle was parked there.
"I told you not to park in that handicapped spot."
Then Licker starts eating the crew. She's a man eating plant.

The head corn husker has a vision of him gardening. But the field is full of live human heads. Then Licker takes Sieve's remains and makes Stain's perfect woman. "Meet Rev." She looks great except for some rather unconvincing red hair. But being genetically similar to Sieve, she loves K but not Stain.

Chapter 7 – Ex Sex

7.99 catches a porn flick on the space waves. It's transmitted by a garbage scow carrying category 13 biohazard waste. Sounds bad.

On the Ex, sex is the subject again. Stain begging Rev for it. Stain sends a message out to empty space about what a great lover he is. Rev gets K out of the freezer, "I want to do it," she says. "My sex organ has not functioned for 2,000 years."
[Tell me about it, dude. Having a dry spell myself. Not quite that long. But is seems that way sometimes. Now K, what you want to do is take about a bucket full of vitamin E, plus selected herbs, and mangos. Fix you right up. After that, if Rev can't rev you up, you must be dead. Oh right, you are.]

Stain sees the porn film during the section when they beg for men to come to their planet. The truckers hit some black ice and the tanker crashes into them. They get the biohazard 13 stuff in the cabin. Then a giant bug heads right for them. Or are they hallucinating? The crew is two men and one woman. For now.

The Ex snaps up the garbage scow as a snack. The crew gets out and climbs Ex's stomach walls.

Upstairs, Rev finally decides she has to have it. Even with Stain. But it turns out what the Bio 13 does is reverse everyone's sexuality. Physically. Then it kills you.

So Rev and Stain finally get together. But she's the male and he's the female. Then Ex gets rid of the Bio 13 and everyone goes back to normal. Well, normal for them. As they fly away, a call comes in, "Emergency, this is the planet Porno calling for men. We must have men! Any men will do."
Stain says, "No way I'm falling for that again."
The camera reveals that this time the message is real.

Chapter 8 – Welcome to the Robot Arms

Not a hotel for robots, the flying robot arms that Man Treed invented. They take all matter nearby and make more robot arms. And 7.99 lost his mind. He has a piece of human brain tissue. He's back but the folks have taken off in a Fly. [So why are the robot arms destroying everything? Well, it's a hobby. Got to keep busy. Here's a thought, somebody could teach them arm wrestling.]

Ex throws his engines into reverse to knock out the arms. The crew calls up Man Treed. He says, "I'm going to destroy all humanity. I'll save you for last. After all, you helped create me."

Chapter 9 – Patches in the Sky

It's the same old story, Stain D. Wheedle finds a place where dreams come true. And what does he dream of? Jiggle Otter, the cannibal queen. Moral: A loser is always a loser.

We see a guy in a modest space cruiser landing at Narco Lounger World, 'Where Your Dreams Come True.' He trades a robot arm for a jolt. He tells the burnt out proprietor, "There are patches in the sky."
"Whatever, dude."

Grubby Mook is the burnt out proprietor. Stain lets Jiggle Otter take control of his dream. A caveat, if you die in the Narco Lounger, you die all over. And, it's an old war surplus machine. Sounds like a nightmare. So that the series can continue, they get out somehow. But patches are eating the universe. And he eats real fast. It's the old geometric progression.

Chapter 10 – Stain Had a Hat On

Not only are galaxies vanishing, Stain lost his hat! Rev takes a shower. Stain wanders in, "looking for his hat." [Us guys like to have a hat on.] Rev doesn't reveal as much as Sieve, but she doesn't need to. Of course Stain says, "The universe is coming to an end, so how about it?"
She says, "We'll talk when it's down to one day left."
"I knew you'd come around."

Ex says there's a giant web in space. He is afraid. Stupid Stain can only think of his hat. There's one day left. Ex is caught in a great, intelligent web. Rev goes to Stain and says, "Well, here I am. I said you could have me when there's one day left."

"Do you feel like a giant web has caught you? Get Web Away today! It's guaranteed to either free you or make you think that you're free. So you win either way."

Chapter 11 – The Inevitable Musical Episode

[Every show must have one since 'Buffy.'] Though K's planet died eons ago, a sort of automatic playhouse travels around reenacting the history of the Bruin Gee. They had "perfected" their lives so that they lived forever. But, only as long as they stayed home. K and a few other "young" ones go to fight the Shadowy. The others are killed later. 'Better to go out with a bang,' said K. [It's not as bad as some musical theater.] K puts on glad rags and joins the troupe. Rev throws on a black wig and joins in. Stain is inspired to fight Man

Treed instead of running to the other universe. Moral: Avoid musical theater at all costs!

Chapter 12 – Find Him First

So Stain, the Average Man, decides to stay and fight, but where is Man Treed? Got to find him to fight him. But someone, in an ancient Bruin Gee ship, answers the call. But he's dead. Rev gives him the kiss of life. If anyone can wake a dead man, she can. His name is Poison. Big muckety muck under He's Shadowy. Says Man Treed was his best student. Poison is in bad shape. Carries a suitcase which performs most of his bodily functions. In a very disgusting way.

He says, "Let's snag a robot arm and I'll reprogram it to shut down the system. But first, Rev, take off your clothes. I must make a small insertion. With this." He holds up a needle. He takes control of K. "Share your liver with me, Rev."
She says, "I haven't heard that line before." So they share a plate of liver and onions. Whew! He neutralizes the robot arms.

So I guess that's it. No arms, no harm. But they have Man Treed treed. Poison says he can use Stains's body to join Rev in a better way. Luckily they are interrupted by finding Man Treed's tree.

Him and Poison have a big battle of insults. Then Man Treed kills Poison. [Bit of a 'six of one, half dozen of the other' situation.]

Chapter 13 – The End of the Universe

[How's that for a title?]
Stain says, "Let's turn the robot arms against each other."
The arms attack. Rev picks up a human thigh bone to use as a weapon. [What next, will she dance around an obelisk?] Licker is back. Or was always there. The arms have killed her pod. 7.99 is attached to a robot arm. He fights off the other arms handily. So they replicate him. It's brains versus brawn in the greatest arm wrestling match of all time! Licker says she can find Man Treed with her dream sensing sense.

Licker slips in and grabs Man Treed. The arms get her. But did she kill him? She slowed him down enough. So a plant saves humanity. But the universe will implode because all the mass is close together now. Everyone says their goodbyes. [So how do they explain the next two seasons?] Oh, they're just popped back into the Twilight Zone, which is what they call our universe.

But Man Treed got into 7.99 and attacks Rev. Licker wakes Stain. [Isn't she dead? Maybe she's in man eating plant heaven, along with Morticia's Cleopatra.] K shoots the arm and Rev crushes the Man Treed chip under her foot.

Chapter 14 – Warm & Wet in the Twilight Zone

[They managed to lure Nigel Bennett away from 'Forever Knight' with their, 'Just say no to contact lenses' policy. "And I want to be a prince," he said. "See what we can do about that," they said. And the rest is history.]

7.99 activates. His sled is rusty. The organic folks are all frozen. 7.99 falls in a hole.

We see Nigel Bennett, excuse me, Prints [Isn't that a dog's name?] flying a be weaponed dirigible. Looks like 'The Road Warrior' took to the air. He pours himself a thimble of water and drinks it. So, not gasoline, but water, is the scarcity here. They board the Ex and look around. A Fly fascinates them. The ship seems dead and deserted. A sound of mourning. It's 7.99.

"Bring me to Rev!"
"So she's the important one?"
"Yes."
Prints tosses 7.99 down a shaft. They find the frozen folks and push a random button. Stain D. Wheedle awakens. He says the Ex is just a big bug that wants to eat. Prints says, "Show me some clips of previous shows. We must familiarize a new audience and bring the fans up to speed after the summer hiatus."
"Okay."

7.99 is now in love with K, not Rev. I suppose he rebooted and saw K first this time. Prints plans to use the Ex to conquer Wet, the other planet. And Rev lost her red wig and went back to her actual blonde hair. She tells Prints he has the key. Prints set him to slave labor with a device which will kill Stain if he stops working.

So one planet is really warm and the other is very wet. They pass close enough for balloonists to go from one to the other. Stain and Rev end up on Warm. K goes to Wet looking for Rev. He hijacks a war balloon and a native of Wet. They fly to Warm, and Maybe, the Wet native, shoots Prints in the chest with an arrow. The Prints is dead, is there a king? Queen, Jack, Joker, Ace?

Poor Ex is starving. But he could destroy one last planet. But which one? Warm or Wet? Rev turns lizard and rolls into the control room. To stop Stain from ordering the destruction of Wet, she smothers him with her breasts. What a way to go. She lets him breathe now and then. The planet is safe.

Chapter 15 – Funny Bunny

We meet Bunny, of Wet, who later is a human of Earth. As is Prints. [Well, if you're going to break the rules, why be picky? I'm starting to think this is fiction anyway.]

Now Maybe shoots Prints again. You can't keep a bad man down. Speaking of a down man, Stain D. Wheedle, who never got any, is getting plenty. He has three insatiable women straddling his already exhausted body. Then two more come in. Apparently the native men there can handle such excesses.

One of whom is with Rev. Then K comes in. He's alive! [I'm thinking the planet Wet is Heaven and Warm is Hell.] The war bell rings. And there's K, still dead. And alive too. He's two, two, two K's for fun.

Chapter 16 – Gorgonzola

K Dead and Bunny and Rev and K Live are chasing the bad guys in a Fly. Between the planets it's double dusk. That's when a lot of young folks jump rope in creative ways. No wait, that's Double Dutch.

They all crash land on the deserts of Warm. They run into some little creatures wearing robes that lead them to an underground place. Then Froufrou and Magic Marker Chin have a pointless conversation.

K Dead gives Bunny a piggy back ride. Or is that gives Piggy a bunny back ride? They find a crashed balloon. "I hear Oz is nice." They stupidly pick up Froufrou and Black Stripe. So K Live shoots Black Stripe. They start talking philosophy. Is there life after death? Well, you just wake up and there you are. There are no children on these planets. [So who drops bubblegum on the sidewalk? Who goes to a swimming pool and screams repeatedly for no apparent reason?]

Froufrou thanks K in that very annoying way of his. He's one of those sleazy guys that can never be trusted. Like Richard Nixon, only less classy.

They crash into a convenient building. Turns out K Live is Prints in disguise. He and Froufrou are about to kill Stain. Rev rolls in and stops them. Stain kills Froufrou. Hooray! [I get the feeling that Prints is the 'Prints of Darkness.' You know, Beelzebub. Now that's one heck of a monicker, "Beelzebub, if you want to leave the room, raise your hand and ask permission, Beelzebub." "Yes, Ma'am." Last name probably Smith. The Smiths like unusual first names because Smith is so common. Like Smith Smith.]

Stain and Rev get into a building, Not Okay Town, where everyone talks and acts like characters out of 'Alice in Wonderland.' Cute in a child's story but not so good in reality. Hey, there's Man Treed! Or at least the same actor. Stain and Rev buddy up with him as the least of the evils.

K arrives. He rescues a woman. She says, "I bet you think you're a big deal, rescuing folks and all?" She goes on and on like that. K walks away saying to himself, "There's just no pleasing some folks."

K finds the other two. "Oh good, you can save us."
K says, "I don't know. After all this stuff lately, I just don't feel right. Sort of out of sorts. Out of kilter. Not feeling myself."
"What can we do?"
"Pull out my control rod. It's between my legs."
Rev says, "I'll do it."
That's a long rod. What do you do with an 'out of alignment' 6,000 year dead, assassin? [They drifted for 4,000 years in the Twilight Zone before ending up half way between Warm and Wet.]

Chapter 17 – Dead Lawyers

K does a belly flop from the tall tower of Not Okay Town. A couple of scavengers scavenge him. They take K to Hung Town, Land of Lawyers, where every jury is a hung jury. K says, "I'd rather be thrown from the high tower." Since that is the usual punishment, eventually they do so. But first, "Are you an assassin?"
"I have killed mothers without babies, round yon virgins, the lame, the gimpy, those with charley horses, shin splints, that achy feeling–"
[Only a 6,000 year dead assassin could outtalk a room full of lawyers. Especially after he grabs the head guys's throat with his Batarang.]

Stain and Rev descend 39 steps into the intertown subway. "Two ticket to paradise." But the ticket booth is empty. And there's no train. Never was. Stain is grabbed by the free medical service. It's free because it's unwanted.

They go to Garden Center where there are only female gardeners. Stain says, "This is my kind of place. Tell you what, you take the key and the Ex and go. I'll stay here." K plants himself in the rich earth. "What a nice place to decompose," he says.

Of course the gardeners have no interest in Stain. "But we can grow you a plant for this sex thing you keep going on about. We take the image from your mind." This is an extremely feculent garden so it only takes a couple of minutes. And there she is – Carmen Miranda. Oh, it's Licker in a funny hat. Licker licks the gardeners. And after she licks you, there's nothing left.

The Prints of Darkling takes Rev on a trip down memory lane. Her least favorite road. So they throw her off the balloon. With a rope attached.

THE END FOR NOW

DISPARATE HOUSEWARES (Desperate Housewives)

[The complete set finally arrived. I can take a break from 'Lexx.' Good show but I'm almost certain it's not based on a true story. Now these housewives of Hysteria Lane, they're for real. Perhaps all these stories would be spread out amongst hundreds of real women instead of four or five, but still.]

As you may recall, unless I skipped over it, Coos N. Mare had a gun pointed at her by that crazy boy from across the street. [When will they put airbags in those things?] The narrator, that lady that played Ellen on 'Seinfeld,' remarks about a woman who had been drinking too much for years. Coos N. tackles the young lunatic while Plumber just stands there, and his large dog, Dumbo, barks uselessly. Coos N. wrestles the gun away. The idiot dog bites her leg. Coos N. stumbles and pulls the trigger. The bullet breaks the bottle of booze in the lady's hand across the street. She looks skyward and says, "When I asked for a sign, I was just kidding! Can't you take a joke?" During the fracas, the young psycho runs away. Welcome to Hysteria Lane!

Coos N. busted her lip so she mumbles, "He wad wading dare do gill ewe."
"Huh?"
She takes out the cotton, "He was waiting there to kill you."
But Plumber says to the cop later, "It was just an accident. She was cleaning my gun and it went off."
"Uh huh. I'll file this under "the rug.""
"Thanks."

Big John shows up at Paella's place. With a gym bag. "Now your husband is in prison . . . "
"Because you told him we were having an affair! Get out!"

In the 4-5 kids house, they move so fast they're hard to count, Mother Samantha is nervous about taking Derwood's place at McMan and Tate while Dobbin stays home with the kids for a change.
"You'll do fine, Hon; you have more brains than the rest put together."

For whatever twisted reason, Mrs. NRA waits till precisely 9 a.m. before calling her friends with news of her husband's death. Remember, he got his prescriptions from his wife's quondam lover? [I know I'm misusing quondam, get off my back!]

Naturally NRA is acting crazy. Rex, the ex alive hubby's mother, comes roaring up in a cab. She's hanging out the window like a dog. She throws herself on the perfectly coifed NRA and weeps.

Paella visits prisoner hubby. He refuses to talk to her. On the way out, he says, "I want a paternity test."

NRA, Breed Bandicoot, [Such an ordinary name I forgot it.] who lost her husband yesterday, goes to welcome the new folks to Hysteria Lane. "Hello, Mrs. Apple Pie, I'm Breed Bandicoot, welcome to Hysteria Lane." [Hey, it's Mrs. Whatsit from 'A Wrinkle in Time.'] And her son, Mammoth [Cause he's big, not because he's wooly or shaped like an elephant, man.] Oh here we go, Breed says, "I hear yo're a pianist. Our church lady got her bottle broken by a sign from above so she's taking a sort of vacation–"
"I'd be happy to be roped into playing."

I knew it! As soon as Breed leaves, Mrs. Whatsit says, "Pretending your dad's dead? But what if he drops in?"
"From Mars?" [I'm guessing. At the border of Hysteria Lane the sign says, 'Ye who have no secrets, don't stop here. Serenity Lane is the place for you. Just up the road, when you see the old oak tree

that was knocked down by the big storm and isn't there anymore, turn left about a mile before that. Can't miss it.]

Coos N. gets one of those fake security signs. In fine print at the bottom it says, "Do not look this up online. We're really a really real service. Really!" The large print says, "This Property Protected by Really Good Security. 'We're the real thing, really. Not one of those, 'Just buy the sign and hope no one looks it up' things."

Paella tries to get a paternity test result so she can photo shop it to show her husband. She talks with another patient, "I got a lesbian's egg implant. Now my husband thinks our child will be born gay." [Have you considered psychiatric help?]

Oh . . . the psycho kid is actually the Plumber's son. Of course. Naturally. Huh? So Snooze N. breaks up with him.

At the funeral, Mom put Rex in his prep school tie, a ghastly bright orange color, and a teddy bear next to him in the coffin. [I mean he was relatively young but that's ridiculous.] They start to close the coffin, "Wait!" yells Breed. [I knew it. Those who hold it in all their lives, those neat freaks, they're the ones that crack. And they crack hard and loud and wide open!] She walks down the aisle, "Give me your tie." She picks up dead hubby, takes off the orange monstrosity, slips the tie around his neck. Ties it, "You look wonderful." She marches out. [Better than digging him up later.]

[Later, they dig him up anyway.] Merely Alice kidnapped the Plumber's kid and raised it as hers. Oh, and murdered the mother. "No wonder she offed herself," says Snooze N. as the four musketeers walk away. "After all, what do we know about our neighbors? If they keep a neat yard, that's good enough." [That's why my yard looks atrocious. Bad yard, good person. Nothing to hide. And don't trust guys that mow their face either. An honest man grows a beard. Case closed.]

[Well, not Mars, he's chained in the basement. These folks will fit right in at Hysteria Lane.]

Chapter 2 – Here We Go

She comes home from work to find filth. "Clean it up, house hubby." [Hey, it's Raj's dad from 'Big Bang.' He's the dry cleaner.] Mother in law causes trouble at the dry cleaner's. [Hubby's gone, get rid of her, is what I say.] It's a grief war. Physics grieves loud and constantly. Breed broods. Obviously each is wrong.

She wants fresh sheets, he doesn't. She tries to make the bed with him in it. She goes to "sleep" on the couch. Or to watch a rat movie. [The bad kind, not 'Ratatouille.'] So is she going to "rat" the house? She brings a rat home from the pet store. Lets it loose in the house. [Sounds like something I'd do. If I didn't have cats. And a gecko and a hawk moth. The moth larva was supposed to be a meal for the lizard. Now I've put a small hummingbird feeder in there for the moth. Want next?]

Snooze Ann hears noises coming from the new lady's house. Mrs. Whatsit says, "That's Mammoth, he's always working on something." We hear the noise. Then Mammoth walks up the street. Oops. Mrs. Whatsit says, "Say, did you ever see 'A Wrinkle in Time?' I'm Mrs. Whatsit. I have magic powers. Don't mess with me."

Eke, here comes the killer pharmacist. He asks her out. No, they hug. Mom peeks out the window.

Speaking of eke, the rat worked. He saw the rat sitting at the table, eating caviar with a silver spoon. But, the rat failed to use his serviette. Atrocious manners!

They're going to dig him up anyway. She could have waited to change his tie. Mom in law told the fuzz she was hugging the pharmacist. She throws mom in law out. She goes off hanging out the cab window like a dog.

Breed takes a lie detector test to see if she killed her husband. The guys asks her, "Are you in love with your pharmacist?"
She says no. The monitor jumps into the red. He asks again, "No!" The red lines nearly jump out of the top of the monitor. Her brain wave patterns spell out, "She's lying! Put the cuffs on her, quick!" [I guess that will be the new computer dating, discover your feelings with a lie detector.]

Mom brings home The Pill Man for dinner. Mom coerces teenage boy to attend. When mom leaves room, boy says, "So tell me, have you ever actually been with a woman? As man of the house, I'm responsible for my mom's happiness. You're obviously not a player. Have you ever even been in the game? My mom and dad had an awesome sex life. I heard through the wall, mom sounded like this," he moans. Mom comes back in. Pill says, "Send him to his room!"
"For what?"
"I can't say." Pill ends up leaving in a huff.

Mrs. Mom killed Mrs. Dingle Berry! First she stuffed her into a trash can. Berry fell off the garbage truck. Then she was run over. Good thing she was imaginary.

Working Mom, to get her mind off her recent murder spree, takes her uptight boss out to a bar. Helps her hook up. She's in a very good mood next morning. And in the same clothes.

Snooze N. has a great book agent, Loony Mon. She says, "I'm getting a little behind in my work. " He says, "I'm opening my own agency, what with the embezzling and all."

Paella stars on a nude website. Breed Bandicoot is picked up for DUI. What next? Instead of Hysteria Lane it should be the intersection of Misdemeanor Lane and Felony Avenue.

Snoozin' tries to pick up a doctor. He gives her a cat scan. He is up all night trying to figure out her "disease." [It's mental, dude.] But she does have a wandering spleen. You've got to sit that spleen down and give it a good talking to.

[It's nun wrestling! Just like on the film, 'Wallace & Gromit: Curse of the Were-Rabbit.'] Paella gets a nun shipped off to Alaska. When she finds out they have a knock down drag out in the nave. The real issue is will she give hubby a baby? He chooses her, she says yes, then they settle on adoption.

Breed says, "My pharmacist killed my husband."
"I hope you got a new pharmacist."

OMG! Snoozin's ex married her again so she could sink her floating spleen on his insurance. Eating Brick, his girlfriend, saw the ring and prenup and jumped to conclusions. Meanwhile, the rejoined exes are thinking maybe the old flame has merely died down to embers. [There's a thing called honesty folks, look into it.]

[IT'S CAROL BURNETT! You know it's a good show when big stars start "dropping in."]

So Moms Maybe is instant messaging with hubby. The boss says, "Tell me what to say to my wife to get things cooking again." She gives him some hints. He's called out of the office. He says, "Go on, you're doing great." So Mom is soft core porning the boss's wife.

Now Mr. Solstice got the maid pregnant. Well, him and his wife, Paella. They said, "She's always hanging around. And she has this womb just gathering dust."

The murderer's neighbor is collecting her own blood. She calls the police, "My neighbor said he's going to spill all eight, um, seven pints of my blood." [Helpful hint: Always count your blood bags BEFORE placing fake emergency calls.]

Eating Brick is attacked by bees because she burned Snoozin's house down.

Mom follows hubby to Atlantis City where he claims to have business. Yeah, funny business.

Eating Brick is in the hospital. Or is it Quasimodo? She was stung by several bees, which she claims were directed by Snoozin'.

Uh oh, little Chow Maid made Solstice a roast beef sandwich. Secret from Paella.

Breed Bandicoot drops her son in the middle of nowhere. Her daughter runs away. She neatly packs a bag and goes to the loony bin to check herself in.

There's blood in the guy's house. In the back of his car is two lady fingers. No, not cookies. Talk about crazy, Bebe cut her own fingers off.

Yikes! A dead lady is walking around! Old Mary Ellen from 'Seinfeld.' Now the dead Mary Alice of 'Desperate Housewives.' Oh, it's a flashback.

[Hey! It's Sheldon Cooper's mom!] Her and Killer Dentist are some new denizens of Murder Mystery Lane. His name is Whoreson Hogs.

Oho, Snoozin's got herself a smoothie with an accent. He gives her a Rolex watch. But when she looks at it closely it says, 'Bowlegs.'

Naturally Breed Bandicoot gets engaged to Whoreson Hogs, the new murderer on Murder Mystery Lane. [If you don't have at least one felony to your credit, you are snubbed there.] The girls ask if he's good in bed.
"We're waiting until after the wedding."
Paella bursts out laughing. Breed isn't joking. "You're serious! You wouldn't buy a car without a test drive?"

They say she's 'Snoozin' on her feet.' Her and Doctor Knock Off are visiting a coma patient. "They were out of coffee so I got us smoothies."
"I wouldn't mind having some real food," he says, taking the flowers to get water, "like a date."
Snoozin' whips around, dumping her smoothie all over his wife in the bed. She throws a blanket over her to hide it.

That Breed is working her way up. From a mentally unbalanced pharmacist to a completely unhinged dentist. [What next, a surgeon named Jack T. Ripper?] But, the delusional dentist is more of a neat freak than she is. She drags him off to bed.

Breed runs to a doctor. "I think I had a small stroke!"
The female doctor says, "My dear, you just had your first orgasm."

Curling Biggie drops in, "I was Whoreson's neighbor." [I think I missed a bit. Did she witness a murder or two?] "Killed his 1st wife," she says.
He says, "Go back to east Texas. You've caught insanity from your son, Sheldon Cooper."
"Shelly's not crazy, I had him tested."
The others think, 'He'll fit right in here.'
[Shirley these people realize that there's at least one major crime per household on their street? And yes, I'm calling you Shirley.]

Of course Breed decides to marry Deadly Dentist. Breed Bandicoot marries Whoreson Hogs so now she's Breed Hogs.

Sheldon Cooper's mom goes berserk with a gun in a grocery store. [Are we surprised?]

[It's Special agent Dale Cooper from 'Twin Peaks' as Whoreson Hogs. Hey, any relation to Sheldon Cooper? Whose mom was shot down like a dog, by the way. She went to confront her husband after his affair with Slutique, the French stewardess with a gun in a crowded store and was shot down by the new guy that Moms Maybe thinks is a predator though he claims to have collected all those toys to give to charity but what about photos of boys in bathing suits but he is a swim coach . . . where was I?]

Now Mook the Plumber is arrested for murdering Slutique. Wasn't she that grocery guy's mistress? Anyway, he found a wrench with one of those paper labels on a string saying, 'The Slutique murder weapon. Remember to dispose of.'

Poor grammar,' he thinks. His Grammar was also arrested for monkey wrenching a stewardess named Slutique. Runs in the family.

Moms is causing a riot by saying Toy Boy is a major perv. His ill sister crashes out. On the other hand, this is Murder Mystery Lane. He probably paved the basement with corpses. [Make for rather uneven footing, wouldn't it?]

[It's Eve of 'Northern Exposure!' The Demented Dentist's even crazier mother. You could knock me over with a feather! I mean a gigantic, heavy feather. Perhaps from a griffin.]

Creepy Guy says to Moms, "Now you've killed my sister, I'm free to pursue my "hobby."
"I hate people that make "air quotes,"" she says.

[Oh, I got the wrong one. Dentist's Mother is Dixie Carter of 'Designing Women.' Alma Hogs, Dentist's "dead" wife, sits in a car and talks with Dixie. Hey, isn't the dentist's dead wife dead? It's mystery wrapped in an enigma surrounded by another synonym I can't recall!]

Oh, the dead wife was merely missing. She snagged him by getting pregnant. But the newborn, being precocious, said, "I'm getting out of this screwed up family right now." And went off hitching across the country. He ended up having a nice life in a pueblo. So Alum's trap was sprung. She said to herself, "I might as well take that 'Northern Exposure' job." And took off without leaving a note.]

Eating Brick is seducing the ex Mr. Paella. To do so she's stooping to honesty. [What a low down dirty trick.]

[It's Roz of 'Frasier.' She's a caterer.] The boy who isn't a twin, House Rolls, finds a body in Mrs. Clutches's freezer. He thinks, 'I can get all kinds of loot over this.' Maggoty Gully, the caterer, is set up by Snoozin' with Mook. Mook waxes nostalgic over his prison days. Mook has regained his memory and is back in love with Snoozin'. He was in a coma next door to Lord Fauntleroy's wife, Plain.

The four star chef is tempting Mrs. Mom at hubby's pizza joint. Meanwhile, the new daughter, from the crazy lady who was thankfully shot dead by Sheldon Cooper's mom in the grocery store, reads to Daddy Maybe from the paper, "Thanks to the new chef, who is probably seducing the owner's wife right now, is now the area's hottest eatery in the contiguous 48 states, including North Dakota."

Paella's new boyfriend, Running For Mayor, is photographed in the elevator, going down with her. But the power was out. If you get my drift. The press is vilifying the candidate when Paella steps up to the podium, says he had just asked her to marry him, "And I was celebrating our love. He was protecting my honor, but I am stepping forward."
"Did you say yes?"
"Yes."
[A few years later, she gets him elected President of These United States. Except for North Dakota which seceded from the Union because of too many jokes made about them by comics and even a lowly parody writer. "That was the last straw," a spokesmodel said.]

The candidate's name is Auld Lang. [His parents were big drunks so they named him after their favorite song sung every New Year's Eve.]

So Eon, the laird, gets on his white horse and nobly rides back to England to let the better man have the "prize," Snoozin'. But Mook doesn't know that, so he takes off to climb Mount Doom. Snoozin' hares off after him. Will she win her dream man? Or get eaten by a bear? She was about to smear on a honey facial but luckily a park ranger said, "Don't smear bear food on your face." She's not eaten yet but is lost. She decides to get eaten by a mountain lion instead.

[It's a Masher, the one that was married, um, Mike Farrell as Captain B. J. Hunnicut. He would never tell what his initials stood for. Let's guess! Barsoom Jumbo Hunnicut? Barrabas Jambalaya Hunnicut?]

At Paella's wedding, Eating and Raoul break up. Paella overhears B J and the bear saying, "Now you've got the Latino vote. You can use her to get the governorship." She runs into Raoul and kisses him in her wedding dress. [How he fit into her wedding dress, we'll never know.]

Mama Breeding Hogs is pregnant and so is her daughter. [Is that catching, like measles?] They bundled her off to a Swiss nunnery. Then what, claim Mom had fraternal twins? Oh, she gets ready to bathe and removes her belly. It's the old switcheroo, pretend the kid is hers. [That is going to be one confused kid.]

Creepy! Plumber Mook Dolphin gets an emergency call from a Miss Sooky Sizemore saying her terlet is jest about to explode. But when he gets there, he's ambushed by a wedding.

Mrs. Senator's ex comes in on her wedding night, "Let's run away together." Eating became poorly hung, by her own hand. Raoul says he can't leave her now. [Once again I say, give honesty a try, you just might like it.]

Snoozin' has her special man now so she goes on and on about how something must be wrong. She says dramatically, "This marriage is doomed," and rushes from the room.

Chapter 3 – Oh My God! New Neighbors!

In Murder Mystery Lane, you have to figure they're murderers at the very least. It's a lady that lived there before and she's got that crazy Nathan Fillion along as "her husband." [Everything about this show should be in quote marks because nothing is ever as it seems.] "He" is a "doctor." Their beautiful teenage girl comes in. "Hey, remember Julienne?"
"Um, a type of French fries?" [Brain fried is more like it.]
"No, Julienne, my daughter, you spent every waking moment together?"
First thing the new, but former, resident says is, "That pine tree will have to go." That's Breed Hogs's favorite tree. It's gonna be a clash of the titans.

Snoozin' goes in for a "check up." Her regular doctor is busy, "But if you don't mind the new guy." In walks that crazy Nathan Fillion. And what kind of doctor is Fillion filling in for? A gynecologist. She wants to run but she's already in the saddle. He keeps saying, "Relax." Then he mentions menopause!

The new lady is called Muriel Cigars. It's the same old story, her friend doesn't want to admit to having cancer and ends up ralphing in her purse from the chemo. Welcome back to Hysteria Lane. [You know what is a popular choice for cancer patients? Cooking meth! Get yourself a black porkpie hat, steal a motor home, and you're all set. Be sure to pick up one of our handy handguns on your way out.]

Eating Brick shows up for the big barbeque. She assumes the party is for her. Eating is trying to guilt Raoul into marrying her. Paella marches over to have a few words with him. They make out behind the car.

Such a common mishap, Breed goes to get a napkin for hubby and accidentally impales her fake baby belly with a shish kebab skewer.

She walks away. Mrs. Clutches sees this and starts screaming. They pretend it was a prank done on purpose.

New Psycho Mom is berating Moms Maybe about some project and finally she whips off her wig and says, "I have cancer." Her friends see this. They berate her for hiding it. [It's the Berate Moms Maybe Gala Invitational! This new semi-annual event will be celebrated every other year right here in Murder Mystery Lane!] They make a Musketeer swear, no more secrets. Uh huh. Except for Paella's affair with her remarried ex, Breed's fake pregnancy, and Snoozin's menopause, sure, no more secrets.

Speaking of secrets, New Girl doesn't remember anything about her former life there. Snoozin' Junior says, "Well, tell me your first memory."
"Well, after getting out of the pod, we disposed of my human body. Oh wait, I'm not suppose to tell any human about that. Hey I know what would be fun. Let's take a nice nap."

Dr. Fillion comes to see Snoozin', "Not only are you not about to start menopause, you're pregnant."

Chapter 4 – The Relatively Innocent Crime Spree

Raoul and Paella are playing the horizontal rumba when Eating comes looking for him. Paella pretends to see him enter her house. She goes there, he speeds around several back yards, knocking over barbeques and such. Then he borrows a kid's skateboard, grabs Eating's car in the classic skooched down position made popular by 'Back to the Future,' hits the curb, rolls, runs to the back door, which is locked. Breaks in. Thus the relatively innocent crime spree. That was fun. Should be the newest Olympic sport. Call it the Dodging-obstacles-to-get-into-the-house-to-fool-one's-pretending-to-be-suicidal-girlfriend-to-be-with-one's-remarried-ex-wife-athon.

Oops, Eating Brick finds out about Raoul's offshore account. She says, "Marry me or I tell the IRS about it." Raoul goes to that skanky pizza place, you know the one, run by Moms and Pops Maybe? He talks to someone about his problem, pushes over an envelope bulging with cash. The camera slowly reveals, the sheriff of Werewolf Village! Raoul is going to have his girlfriend torn apart by a werewolf! [Isn't that one of the "don'ts" in the 'Handbook of Dating Do's and Don'ts'?] [Oops, never mind. I was watching with my glasses off. Raoul hired an ordinary hitman. Where do you find those guys, in the Yellow Pages?]

Chapter 5 – The Great Almost Didn't Happen Charades Party

Everyone begs off Snoozin's lame charades party she insists on having every year. But one says, "Maybe we can get "the Great" liquored up and pump her for information. [They call the new lady "the Great" because her name is Catherine. Also, she likes horses and has the attitude of an empress.]

Moms Maybe's lost her appetite. Old Granny Maybe says, "Let Granny score you some kick ass chronic. I used it when I was on chemo."

[Plumber says their kid has to be a Colts fan. So this is the part of Indiana located in Southern California.] Snoozin' asks Breed for her gyno's number. "That Nathan Fillion is so creepy. Did you see him on 'Buffy?'" But since Breed is faking her pregnancy, she picks a random doctor out of the Yellow Pages. The ad says, 'Come on down to Honest Abe's Gynecology Clinic and Bait Shop.'

Grandma sent Maybe Junior off to score some primo weed. But how to get Moms to take it?

I wasn't far off, the clinic Breed sent Snoozin' to has a cigaret machine in the lobby. On the steel grilled window it says, 'Lotto sold here.'

So, Granny makes pot brownies. Granny sends the boy up to beg Moms to eat just one. That's an effective drug delivery system.

Moms is watching cartoons with the kids and laughing. Then she goes to the party. "It's the charades ninja!" She kicks over a lamp. She's way too stoned to give charades clues. Finally she mimes hanging and points to Eating Brick. "Hang 'Em High."

Chapter 6 – Crotch Crickets

Eating Brick's gyno, who inexplicable fails to have a cigaret machine, or to sell Lotto tickets, finds crotch crickets "down there." She says to Raoul, "Well, at least we're in a committed relationship. Don't have to make the 'call of shame,' to every partner." Which includes Paella, new wife of His High and Mightiness, Mayor of Crime City. Paella comes up with a plan. She plays naughty nurse and puts anti cricket medicine on the High Chieftain.

Snoozin' is failing to win over the new couple next door. So she steals their dog. The plan is to "rescue" the animal and take it back to the eternally grateful owners. Remember this is Losin' Snoozin's plan. She sticks him in the garage. With the open can of paint her husband left there. The pooch runs out with yellow paint on his paws. Hubby came home and opened the garage door, thus letting the dog out of the bag. [Well, since you asked. The phrase 'let the cat out of the bag' dates back at least to Chaucer's time. Probably much earlier. A roadside sharp would offer travelers a nice "piglet" at a bargain price. Down the road a piece, the travelers would open the sack to find that, unbeknownst to them, a cat had been substituted for the piglet. Thus the old saying: Ye should always check with the Better Business Bureau.] The yellow foot dog leapt up on his owner, who was wearing a $2,000 suit. [I'd get my money back. I mean it's a plain black suit. Besides that it has yellow splotches on the front.]

To get even, the guys put a "tinfoil monstrosity' in their front yard. Psycho Mom says she can get rid of it in one week flat. They paid $24,000 for it. ['A fool and his money, soon are parted,' according to Washington Franklin, author of the book, 'Never Buy a Pig in a Poke,' by William Chaucer.] Then they turn on the water. The metal plates of the fountain make a huge racket.

His Highness put a tail on Paella. Not in the bedroom, a man in a van on the street eating sweets. But before you can recite 'One fish, two fish, red fish, blue,' Paella devises a plan to trick the van man with a bike hike. She has some kids over doing yard work. Kids on bicycles. She pays them off in the house and they run out and ride away. [If you haven't seen the show, Paella is played by a short, slender woman. Easy for her to pass as a child.]

At the No Tell Motel, Paella runs into Big John and his new wife, a hotel heiress, "But not one of the skanky ones," she says.

Psycho Mom gets elected head of the Neighborhood Beautification Society.

Chapter 7 – Cages

Turns out Plumber's father is in jail for murder one. In other news, something dug in Cancer Mom's garden and she goes to the death store for a big bag of poison and a trap. When these don't work, she goes to Breed Hogs for gun advice. "All we're allowed here are air guns. Won't kill it but it will make the critter leave and not come back."

Chapter 8 – Modern Inconveniences

Moms packs up Grandma's things and puts them in the car trunk. At a diner, tries to talk Sis into taking her back. Sis says no. But when she's distracted, Moms opens her trunk with the remote, nips out, puts Grandma's bags in, and vamooses. [That's why I always keep my keyless remote in a separate place. Hanging on a hook by the door at home. When I go out, I have the car key. At home, I may want to open the car for some other purpose than driving. The keys are hidden elsewhere. You've got to be smarter than your tools.]

Mr. Hogs is firmly against circumcision. He sends out instructions in this regard to all hospitals in a two state area. Breed tries to crash a Bris. She cons the moil, "I swear my son will be as good a Jew as I am." [If she's not careful, hubby will run off, join the FBI, and star in 'Twin Peaks.']

The "gun" His Mayorship was reaching for was a sweater. Aha! He planned to kill her with warmth! That fiend! Raoul shows up. They go out to rescue His Eminence. They pick him up, have a few words, he picks up a knife, for Raoul, once again he gets paddle whacked by Paella. This time he doesn't come back up. Now what, push the boat out alone?

Uh oh, Chicago. The bimbo from Gnat Fillion's past has followed him to Murder City. For his silence, Plumber gets a prescription for his pain pills that he swore to Snoozin' he was off of.

[A MUSKETEER! And the star of Shogun, and the Thorn Birds. You know, Aramis. I mean Richard Chamberlain. He plays the estranged hubby of Grandma Chronic.]

Another miracle! His Honorific is found washed up on the beach – alive! The Mayor of Memory Loss has memory loss. Or does he?

Chapter 9 – TWISTER!

Paella says she's hitting the road. Also, there's a tornado at Mount Pleasant. [So now we're in Kansas? I find that Toto unbelievable, Dorothy. This show moves around more than a hyper speed freak.]

Gnat Fillion's crazy stalker rolls in from Chi Town. Breed brings her in for tea. Sybil locks her selves in the bathroom. Which is also the storm shelter.

Mook is now a pill head. Then he throws Snoozin' down the stairs. Sort of. The hospital is crowded. So Mook socks a Doc. Everybody is tornado crazy. [Tornados are small. Wake me when it grows into a hurricane.] Of course all the residents of Hysteria Lane are calm and cool during the storm. [If you believe that, I have some prime real estate to sell you in the heart of downtown Hysteria Lane. Guaranteed to have one murder or less committed on the premises.]

His Craziness shows up with a gun. He and Raoul fight out in the storm. His gets a picket fence picket through the heart. Raoul gets a knock on the head. Eating Brick and Paella make peace so as not to die enemies. But they agree if they live through this they will go right back to being enemies. I mean, let's be reasonable.

The crazy lady, okay, the crazy lady that seduced Gnat Fillion, walks out the front door. Well, she flies out. Good riddance. And good riddance to the psycho mayor.

And the papers with the info on how to get the offshore money blows away in the wind. And then the accountant has the nerve to drop dead.

Raoul goes blind from his injury. Imagine that for Paella, the proud former model.

Chapter 10 – Handicap This!

Only Paella Raoul-Mayor-Raoul would not only park in a handicapped spot because her husband is blind, and sitting at home, but she says to the wheelchair bound guy that complains, "Ha! I have to walk around in heels all day while you just sit and roll around." The guy tries to call the cops, she grabs his phone. Another wheelchair guy rolls up. He goes for help. She pushes the first guy across the lot so she can drive away. She says "Well that's it. It's official. I'm going to Hell."

Next day she puts Raoul in the car to run errands. Her manicure is the last straw. He walks away.

Uh oh, the two alpha females are wrangling over pear versus apple slices in the Waldorf salad. Clear a space and sell some tickets!

Paella and Raoul are getting all gussied up. The Great is taking over everything. The caterer has some dip that went bad. "Could you toss that for me? I'm so rushed." Breed heads out of the kitchen with the spoiled stuff. The Great comes in, "Remember, nothing leaves the kitchen without me tasting it first." She is sick as a dog, but pulls herself to the podium. "And the award goes to, Breed Hogs."

Rick's Place, right next to Moms and Pops Pizza Palace is arsoned. Remember Rick was the guy coming on to Moms. [Hey, isn't Rick's Place in Casablanca? They must have moved it.] Anyway, Pops sneaks back to the award banquet carrying two empty five gallon gasoline cans. "Had a sudden compulsion to fill the lawn mower."
"Didn't you get an electric mower recently?"
"Yeah well, what if the juice goes out like when we had that tornado? Can't have unsightly weeds sprouting up just because of a disaster."
"And where did you get that 'I Hate Rick's' tee shirt. And that 'I Bricked Rick's' hat?"

Raoul gets a seeing eye dog. Paella starts in with, "Can she fetch the remote for Raoul? Or find his keys, turn off the radio, lick up his spills?"
Raoul says, "In her free time she solves crimes with Shaggy and the gang."
"On TV I saw a collie that could push a lawn mower." She storms off.
Raoul says to the dog trainer, "Did I lie?"
"Nope. Wow!"
The dog's name is Roxanne Simone de Beauvoir Grand Champion Foxcliffe Hickory Wind the Third.

Whoreson, after Mook apologized for coercing him into writing a prescription for his addiction, started sleep walking. "I'm sorry for running over you, Mook. I suspected that, some time in the future, if we became acquainted, you might get hooked on pills and coerce me into writing you a prescription," he mumbled incoherently. Probably a meaningless coincidence.

Rocks takes exception to Paella being mean to her husband. So she's a guide/guard dog. Who's top dog now? I don't mean to imply that Paella is a female dog . . .

Later, Paella enters the bedroom, only to find Rocks in bed with her husband. "Oh hail gnaw," she says, "It's me or the dog." He pets the dog. She storms out. [Something tells me this isn't over.]

Meanwhile, Creepy Cop pulls Dullard over for not speeding. "Do you know how slow you were going, Miss? A guy passed you in a wheelchair. From now on I want you to go at least 5 miles over the

speed limit. Everyone else does. By the way, I am your father, Luke."
"I never watched 'Star Wars' so I don't get that reference." [Dullard is the daughter of Psycho Mom, AKA, the Great.]

Paella drops Rocks off at the dog place, "We got a seeing eye monkey instead." She drives away. The dog follows on her scooter. She flips open her phone, "Scooby Roo, me forrow bad grrr. Come whelp."

Dullard says, "We could sneak around to seedy motels and have a father daughter thing without telling Mom." [Ah yes, sneaking around is always the sign of a healthy relationship.]

Reek, of Rick's Place, confronts Pops, who pops him one. The police say not enough evidence. The wife lies to protect Pops. Then he puts both feet in his mouth by saying, "Like I believe you didn't have an affair with him." [I hope he has a comfy sofa.]

Plumber says, "I'm going to forgive Whoreson. After all, it was only a midsized car he hit me with. Not like it was an SUV."
Snoozin' says, "He should go to prison." [He's more the loony bin type.]

The twins tell Moms they burned Rick's. She gives them a severe time out.

Dullard hops in a car with her "father" whom she just met. What a dullard. Of course he did offer her some candy so I guess it's okay.

Justine Bateman comes to rent a room from Paella and Raoul and Rocks. She says, "I'm an art student, mind if I pay cash?"
Raoul smells a rat, and not the one Rocks dragged in. [Generally, 'art student' and 'flat broke' go hand in hand. Maybe she's an art dealer. And by art, I mean drug. Oh right, she was a child star so probably just robbed a liquor store, so that's okay.]

Snoozin', who I just realized is Lois Lane on another channel, so I'm slow on the uptake, so sue me, meets her first husband and 'one of his skanks' at her Lamaze class. He's having a fabulous life, the crumb.

Justine has a man over. Oh, prostitute. Is that better or worse than drug dealer or robber of small businesses?

Aha! The boys started the fire but little Kaley suggested it. She's the mastermind of the gang.

Snoozin' drags an overdressed Mook to Lamaze and they 'put on the dog' to impress the ex. "Hi, My name is Mook and I'm a drug addict."
"Hi, Mook."

Paella gets the gay guy to proposition Justine who slaps his face. Okay, so she's charging for art lessons? Nude modeling? Selling autographs? She says tattoos. Of course, the old in home tattoo parlor.

Interesting, Dullard has different DNA from her parents. Also, her scar from falling off the bike? Gone. [I told you she was a pod person. No wonder she doesn't remember her childhood, pods don't have childhoods, they grow on a vine.]

Action! The dead Gnat Fillion comes back looking for Crazy Cop. Who says, "You let my daughter die like a dog. [I get the distinct feeling a big dog owner has joined the writing staff.] So Dead Gnat stops the killer who says, "I'll make you pay," to Whatsername who shoots him. The ladies set up a story to protect her.

THE END FOR NOW

The Ex (Lexx)

[Well, my shipment of Lexx discs vanished. My advice, use USPS rather than UPS. So I'm going to go ahead and play what discs I have. Anyway, this isn't the kind of show where you need to see every episode.] [Update, I found the discs under something else in the box.]

Chapter 1 – What a Weird Planet

We open with Prints advising the President of the United States on how to communicate with aliens. The Ex has been spotted in orbit. The President tries to talk with Stain D. Wheedle, who is obsessed with finding a planet with friendly females. He gets mad and says, "Ex, blow up that planet!"
Luckily, Rev is now the captain, so Ex ignores Stain's order.

Disembark Prints says to the Prez, "We're clearly under threat. Time to invoke the Engelbert Humperdinck Plan." They send up a couple of multiple murderers to kill the aliens. In a space shuttle.

Ex needs to eat. It eats greens. Green islands, green continents, green planets. It's a big bug with a big appetite. Ex sees the shuttle, "Mm, a snack." Ex eats Paraguay. In other news, Prints's buddy, Regular Jape Reeks, is elected president.

Some UFO nuts discover a giant Fly flying into Earth's atmosphere. The Air Force scrambles some fighters. 7.99 Plus Tax hacks their tracking code and arranges for the missiles to attack their own aircraft.

Back on the Ex, while Wheedle takes pot shots at outlying planets, Prints shows up. [I thought Rev had the key?]

Rev turns into a country western singer. But she's so bad they throw her in prison. [Hey it's that guy from 'Red Dwarf.' The human guy.]

So, say you have a bunch of assassins. Really good ones. What if they get out of line? You need assassin assassins. And that's what K finds in Trance Sylvan Ya. So how is K going to kill the creature that is designed to kill him?

So there's a fake Dracula and Renfield and three Goth girls in the castle. But who is the real power? K is iron maidened. He shrugs it off. Deep in the bowels of the castle, there is a cryo coffin. Inside is K Squared, an assassin assassin. But can K kill the killer killer?

Rev gets to wear some new costumes. [One trouble with science fiction, they often wear uniforms.] Back on Earth, the three weird sisters call upon Stain D. Wheedle. The witches, or images of them, appear on the Ex. They cast a spell to look like Rev, K, and 7.99. Rev dons a black wig. [Xenia Seeberg, I should say.] And K acts like a woman. Stain is discomfited and hops a Fly. Which takes him to the Three in person. They steal K's dodo blood for Void, the Inhaler.

The witch queen awakes. She has a pyramid of hair. Or a cone. She kills the girls. The wages of sin, as they say.

Rev has to find something to help K. 'Only the pure of heart may defeat the evil one.' Void Flies up to the Ex and puts the bite on Stain. Void bites Rev. [Looks like it's curtains for the good guys.] Rev shoves Void into the freezer. They purify Stain's blood with the

Deus Ex Machina device so he becomes 'pure of heart.' And all is well.

Chapter 2 – Hill Valley

The crew of the Ex end up in a typical Earth town. The computer picks Hill Valley, State, as the most average town in the US of A. Green lawns, red meat, and plenty of guns. Let us skip ahead to the climactic scene. A shootout with some FBI agents and random loonies in which each handgun has about 300 rounds of ammo, as in the early Westerns.

But first, they buy a house. With help from above. 7.99 can easily hack any Earth system. They pop K in a freezer. Rev burns some food. They watch TV. But there are problems. The Earth freezing unit is not cold enough for K. Stain says, "I can fix it. I'll have our stiff frozen stiff in a jiff." [A good slogan for cryogenics.]

In the end, though dozens lie dead of gunshot wounds, one young couple finds love. And that makes it all worthwhile. [Right?]

Chapter 3 – The Last Chapter

There's a giant potato headed straight for Earth. [Either that or some cheap special effects.] Even the President, who claimed to be a veteran pilot, must join in the fray. [Okay, what is a fray, exactly? A fracas I've heard of. So a fray would be about $2/3$ of a fracas?]

Prints appears on the bridge of the Ex and brings some bad news. "I am Death. I appear to people just before they die." So who is the unlucky person? Old Ex is over 6,000 years old now. Giant flying bug space ships tend to slow up a bit at that age.

On Earth, the giant potato is attacking. Ex shoots at it but the old fellow is about out. But K says, "'I did not stop for Dudley Death, but he did stop for me.'" The spirit of Emily Dickenson rises up and murders K. "That's for murdering my verse!"

Begone foul spirit! But Dudley Death is a man of his word. Or a personification of his word anyway. He promised to restore K to life, and he does. Just when everyone is doomed.

K enters the enemy asteroid. He sings his death song, 'Yo Ho Ho and a Bottle of Rum.' He dies. Only 8,000 years old. Still a young man.

Floating in the wreckage we see Ex Junior, the newborn baby of the Ex. Rev and Stain say, "Little Ex, find us a new home."

7.99 Plus Tax begins reciting an epic poem that will drag on for 10,000 years. Luckily Emily Dickenson's ghost is still hanging around to watch the show. She throws 7.99 into the engine intake of Ex Junior where he is destroyed.

[And all over the world, science fiction fans say, "Wow! Nobody will ever top this!"]

THE END

IT'S MOSTLY DARK (Forever Knight)

Chapter 1 – Who's That Girl?

"He was brought across in 1228."
"Why I got to go steerage? Don't you old vamps put some money aside for a rainy day?"

Forever is biting Buddha! That's what she called herself. [Who is that girl? She makes me think of Milady of 'The Three Musketeers?' Tamara Gorski! She played Morrigan on 'Hercules: The Legendary Journeys. And on 'Angel' she played an actress who wants to be a vamp so she makes Angel "perfectly happy," get your mind out of the gutter, with a powerful tranquilizer. And when Angel is happy, everyone else isn't.] [Hey! Forever has a camera in his fridge. Right behind the blood bottles.]

So anyway, a guy blows up an airliner with a tiny music box. [What was inside, a tiny nuke?] Everybody dies except one infant who miraculously drops right into Forever's ragtop Caddy. The kid says, "Whew! Somebody get me a milk! Make it a double!"

Gorski is on the Titanic. She has a magic Buddha which will grant one wish. I think Skunky was on the plane. The new girl's name is Detective Tracer Wetly. A passenger is a vampire. Wetly finds him and faints.

Nuttily gets all mad when Forever tells her about the Buddha. Black Jeans is gone too. Who's left? Only Croissant. [Funny, he played Dudley Death on 'Lexx' and here he's the vamp master.] Forever Nightly throws in the towel. He says to the captain [Played by Toto of 'Tin Man.'] "I'm going to go vampire full time. This cop stuff is eating into my eating time."

Forever is packing to move. Nuttily storms in to complain. Is that all she ever does? [She's the only regular left besides Croissant and he's a bit irregular. Bad diet. Come on folks, there's a whole season still to come.]

The captain, Rhesus, has his hand on a piece of candy. Sent by the mad bomber. If he's not careful, soon Rhesus will be Rhesus pieces. Forever flies over to Toto's office. "I got a hankering for some candy, man." He grabs the box and jumps out the window. [There's a little thing called sharing, dude.]

They have New Girl at "the church." [What the heck are vamps doing in a church?] This one vamp claims he was a conquistador. [Yeah sure you were. And I was at the Battle of Hasty Pudding.] "We were brought across by Pocahontas. Then she said, 'See you in the history books,' and walked into the rising sun. What a weirdo."

One of the guys is an inker. He inks 'Vampire Comics' and 'Comic Vampires.' Uh oh, Wetly has a music box.

Chapter 2 – Pop Psych

Nuttily watches one of those god awful pop psychology shows on TV. The shrink says the unhealthy type of love is based on the unattainable. Nuttily makes a moue.

Voucher is the vampire informant working with Detective Wetly. She's going to appear on the Faller Show. Voucher walks up to Wetly, who is now in a miniskirt, "The deal went south. The Fat Man had his gun moll ice Thursday. He took off with the bird for Casablanca."
Then a street punk tries to ice the queen bee with a wicked shiv. Voucher does the kung fu two step and the punk hares it like a hell beast on the rock.

Later, when she dresses herself, Wetly looks like a nun. Faller's assistant set up the hit for ratings. [They say it's a cut throat business but this is ridiculous.] The ass. points a gun at the nun.

She's a nun gun nut, tut tut. Then she shoots Faller instead. "Well, I just wanted to shoot somebody. I'm not picky."

Then Nuttily and Forever kiss and make up. Just like an estranged couple on the Jersey Faller Show.

Croissant has devolved into an announcer for strippers at the 'Raving,' which used to be Black Jeans's club. Here's a new twist, a girl with multiple personality where one of her is a vampire. The other her is not a vamp and has to wonder why she wakes up next to guys with fang marks and no blood. 'Probably just a coincidence,' she thinks.

Chapter 3 – Damned Noisy Lambs!

They got one of those 'eat your liver and spout lame philosophy' guys that Forever Nightly needs info from.

Detective Wetly gets herself hired by that cannibal lady from 'Lexx.' [Is there a lot of cannibalism in Canada? It does get cold up there. I mean think, there's a big winter storm, the roads are impassible, the juice goes out, the family members start giving each other 'that look' and sharpening their knives. It's a fact that every time there's a hard winter, the population drops.] [Well, that takes care of Canada. I'm determined to insult every country, religion, or other group of people on the face of the planet. How about those pygmies, eh? They're so short it's ridiculous. Take some vitamins will ya?]

Oops, this guy doesn't eat people, he stuffs them. He's a taxidermist gone wild!

Tracer Wetly is talking to herself. That's a sure sign of insanity! [Hey wait a minute, I talk to myself. Uh oh. Maybe all those dozens of people were right in what they said about me.]

Wetly finds the 'Sideshow Man.' He cuts folks up and puts their parts in jars like the famous two headed calf of circus sideshows.

Now they're collecting tattooed girls. Got bored with the plain wrapper. Turns out his pen pal, Iris Bulb, is actually Croissant.

Chapter 4 – Forever Nightly Is Shot Dead!

Wait a minute, he's a vampire. Anyway, it's exciting, they rush him into the emergency room. Do all those medical things. But it's too late. "He's dead. Time?"

"He was brought across at 12:28 a.m."
"Are you trying to be funny or something? Get the hell out of my ER!"

Tracer Wetly tries to recall the circumstances. She says, "It all happened so fast."
[FOUL! Illegal use of a used up cliché. Award the other team a free kick. See, I can be international. Just once I'd like a character to say, "It all happened so slowly. I fell asleep in the middle."]

Nuttily Lambskin rushes in as they're about to bury him. She says, "Because of some medical mumbo jumbo and double talk, he seemed to have his head blown clean off but it was actually just a severe hangnail." She turns to Forever, "How are you doing, Bullet Head?"
"Who are you?"
"You have amnesia!"
"Naw, I was just imitating the caterpillar."
Later Forever Nightly is digging into some grub. "You're eating!"
He gets the impression that Nuttily is just plain nutty.

They were ambushed at the parade float warehouse. Suddenly Rocky the Flying Squirrel was there! Doing nothing! Of course, he's a float. But some guy shot Forever Nightly. Tracer Wetly can't remember. She says, "I tried to head him off at the pass but it all happened so fast. It was quiet. Too quiet. The natives were restless."
The other cop slaps her to snap her out of it. "You were hysterical."

Forever noodles around on the piano playing the Moonlight Sonata. He says, "Funny, I get an image of me playing this while some guy writes down the notes. With a quill pen. He was hard of hearing. Named after a large dog in a movie. I remember we took swigs from his 'Fifth' until the 'Ninth' hour. What was his name? Leibfraumilch? Farfegnugen?"
"Well, I'm going to the bait shop toe get vein shrimp."
"What? In think my brain injury is acting up."
"Got to run. Must pick up extra shrimp for Elise."
[Not nice to play word games with someone who just had half his brain blown out.]

Croissant starts to tell Forever about himself but is rudely interrupted by one of those pesky flashbacks. Then Dr. Lambskin shows up. She doesn't want to tell him about the vamp stuff. He says, "What is it? Am I gay?"

"Well . . . " She wags her hand. "I don't know about that, but you're never with a woman. And you're always hanging out with that Creepy Crawly guy from the radio."
He says to her, "Well, there's one way to find out." She's been waiting years for this. [But we're rated PG so we cut to commercial.]

Next morning she's sleeping it off when Nightly goes out for bacon. In the sunlight he turns into frying bacon. After bathing in fire extinguisher mist, he asks Nuttily, "Why do I fry?"
"You also fly. You're a vamp pie, er."
"Do I have to wear a cape and talk with a heavy accent?"
"No, that's myths, mister."
"Hey, I figured it out, bait toe vein, the composer was a shrimper."
"Um, no. You haven't learned much, though you've been a vampire for 767 years."
"Do I get weekends off? Paid vacations?"
"No. But the health benefits are great."
"But only nightly."
"That's rightly. You've been trying to humanize yourself."
"You're nuts, Nuttily, nuts." He rushes out.

At a deserted stockyard, or whatever they have in Toronto– Let me start again. In a deserted stockyard equivalent, Tracer Wetly gets shot at. It was her they wanted all along! Forever Nightly just got in the way! That's a relief. After all, he is the star of the show. But he rescues her anyway.

THE END FOR NOW

DESPERATELY HOUSEFLIES (Desperate Housewives)

[Everything's different! Did I miss something? Pizza Lady's little twins are hosting poker and booze parties at the pizza joint. Snoozin' is with a different guy. [Another 'Tin Man' man, the quondam man himself, the Tin Man of 'Tin Man.' Does anyone out there know what quondam means? Neal McDonough, that is. The Tin Man. Pay attention.] He drops in on this old guy, hands him a huge wad of cash and says, "Get lost." Turns out to be Eating Brick's new husband.

To announce her return [Did she leave? I'm sure I played all the previous discs. Did my mind take a vacation? After all, I'm not a

spring chicken anymore. I'm a summer chicken.] she washes the
car wearing a daring leopard print bathing suit. The ladies rush
over. Eating Brick says to Paella, "What happened to you?"
"I had two children."
"What, for breakfast?"
The Tin Man says, "Let's tone it down, Shnookie Lumps."
AND EATING BRICK APOLOGIZES! Meek as a little lamb. Eating
says, "Sorry. I baked some muffins."

Paella's "little" girl is as big as her mom, and she's only four years
old. Mr. Pizza has a classic car that claims all his attention. Paella
attaches her daughter's leash to the car and forces her to jog.
[Didn't they put Tom Hanks in jail for that in 'Turner and Hooch?'
Only he was a dog. Hooch, not Tom Hanks.]

Poor Paella, says she's lost her beauty over the last five years. Her
nice hubby, Blind Raoul, says, "You're just as beautiful as ever in my
eyes."
"Gee thanks, Mr. Feliciano."

Oh, it was another accident. When Snoozin' killed Mook. [You have
to say, 'Mook is dead,' not just show some vague car wreck when
folks are settling in to watch the show. Oh wait, flashback. Snoozin'
blames herself for killing the other folks. She pushed Mook away
after that. Why they call her Losin' Snoozin'.]

Guy calls up Tin Man, "You're supposed to check in with us in the
Outer Zone once a month, Earth time."
"Aw, I'm back in Kansas now, Wizard. I'm staying away from hot air
balloons. Don't worry."

Chapter 2 – Snoozin's Snoozing

And her young lover, Jackson Pillock, runs into Mook Plumber
picking up the paper. [I'll leave it to the reader to guess who picked
it up.]

Tin Man calls himself Dove Wings, trying to fool everyone. He runs
around doing good deeds like some kind of good deed doer.

Raoul does 'in home' massages. Paella orders him out after seeing
way too much of an elderly man. He takes the country club job as a
tennis pro. [A blind tennis pro? Sure. All he has to say is, "Looking
good, Mrs. Johnson." Even though she looks like a flamingo
throwing a fit. Easier to lie with blind eyes.]

Breed publishes a cookbook under her previous name – Breed Bandicoot. Her husband, says, "Why can't you use my name?"
"Recipes by Mrs. Scummy Sludge?"
"Well, maybe not."

Paella is disinvited from a swanky do. She complains. Breed says, "But Raoul has rubbed too many members." [Okay, he's a masseuse, not a tennis pro. But he is taking up golf. FORE!]

The modern age: Moms Pizza starts internet chatting with her sons under an assumed name. They debate the relative merits of Walt Whitman v. Emily Dickenson with such witty sobriquets as, "Emily Dickenson kicks Walt Whitman's ass!" [All right, so I don't know the meaning of sobriquet. Go stuff it in your quondam.]

Oh my god, Tin Man catnaps Mrs. Clutches cat to coerce her into apologizing to Eating Brick. [Since they're married I guess she's now Eating Man. The girls say she's been a man eater for a long time.] Once more a monster has come home to roost on Hysteria Lane.

The boy take Mom's Yeats to school. [Isn't that illegal? What is a Yeats anyway? Just kidding, I know about old Crazy Yeats, the versifier. Also a card game.]

Whoreson feels left out. "What's wrong with my name for a cookbook, Scummy Whoreson Sludge?"

We might have guessed, Pottery Pizza falls in love with 'that girl on the computer.' HIS MOTHER! Now she'll have to dump her own son. Either that or have a really awkward prom.

Paella tries to take Raoul in the back way to the big party to pretend they're not frozen out. Big mistake.

Moms Pizza is jealous of Breed's book. [So everybody should publish one. On Amazon you can publish your book at zero cost to you. And then try to shame your friends and relatives into buying a copy. It helps if you put at the top, 'This book is dedicated to all the little people who, each in their own small way, contributed, if only by being lucky enough to know me.']

THE END FOR NOW

LA MACHINE (The Machine)

They finally come up with realistic, intelligent robots. 'Finally, we can end the war against China.' [That's an easy prediction. West versus East. But what of the Middle East? As time passes, folks will convert away from oil and coal.] Oh, she's human. They're basing La Machine on her.

"Remove the restraints." She, or it, grabs his arm, sniffs, "You smell sweet." Then he shoves a spider in her face. She doesn't like it. Then they have a guy back up to her. He turns around suddenly wearing a scary mask. She kills him. She freezes. [Who ordered that stupid test? How about a bit of a slower start? Too late for mask man. Moral: Never be a gofer in a high tech secret lab.]

So far the robots are smarter than the humans. La Machine thinks things over for a while and then goes to see The Creator. He says, "I'm busy." She grabs his arm. "Ouch!"

Schooling? Internet? The other robots speak in a distorted voice to each other. [If I was human, I'd be heading for the hills about now.]

A bit of nude interpretive dance. It wants to be an artist, not a killer. It's the old 'what does it mean to be human' bit.

Now she's drawing. That Fool Thompson comes in. "There's a secret file in you. Open it. Install."
"Okay."

Van Gogh sits with his daughter who is gravely ill.

Thompson takes La Machine to see a prisoner. "He killed your mother. He wants to kill Van Gogh."
"So I stop him."
She breaks the guy's arm.
"Kill him."
"No. Van Gogh told me not to kill anymore."

When Van returns later she's hiding under the desk, "I don't like this place." He tells her about vacations at the seaside. He has to prove she's "really alive" or they'll just turn her into a killing machine.

Ah, Van Gogh is scanning his daughter's brain. If she dies, he can recreate her as a robot. And of course she dies.

He's ordered to dumb down La Machine. As he operates, she says, "Please stop. I don't want to die." That Fool Thompson steps in, "We're going to erase your daughter."

Then they order La Machine to kill Vincent Van Gogh. She pulls the trigger but it's not loaded.

Then the tech guy says, "All he removed was the GPS. We can't destroy her remotely."

Then it's robot kung fu action. Guns too. They shoot her about 9,000 times. She says, "That is annoying."

His daughter, in the computer, lives to hang out with "Mother." The camera pulls back to see the "new people" by the sea.

THE END

IT'S ALWAYS NIGHT (Forever Knight)

A woman drives off a bridge. "Let my people go," she says. Or something like that.

Big bible story. The lady had lamb's blood in her. She liked to get her exorcise. I know, demons are lousy drivers.

The exorcist's name is Art Vandelay. He also dabbles in architecture and importing. No exporting. They figure that the devil drove her off the bridge. [The police dispatcher says, "Please be advised. Be on the lookout for one Beelzebub, AKA Mephistopheles, AKA Old Scratch, AKA the Prints of Darkness, AKA the Devil, AKA Satan, AKA Lucifer, AKA the Prints of Lies, AKA Belial, Mammon, Old Nick, Old Harry, The Evil One . . . " Sounds like one of those guys that keeps making up nicknames for himself but the other guys insist on calling him by his real name, Gaylord. No wonder he turned evil.]

Guess what? Rasputin was a vampire. The Mad Mink, they used to call him. Night Knack kills him.

Guy stealing a rat. Woman protests. He throws her down the stairs. [Just another senseless rat stealing death. When will they put air bags in those things?]

Screech, the rat eater, eats the escaped lab rat. [So now what, he turns into a super hero? Rat Man! He scuttles through the night, cleaning up dangerous leftovers. Thank God for Rat Man! "My girlfriend dropped in unexpectedly. To buy some time, I asked her to wait whilst I put my other girlfriend out the bathroom window. My apartment was a huge mess. I turned on the Rat Signal, and soon Rat Man was there. Eating up leftover pizza bits in a flash. I was saved! From minor embarrassment. Thank God for Rat Man! This ad paid for by Rat Man.]

Voucher lets Screech put the bite on him. "Well, you're not a rat, but you'll have to do." The fancy lab rat made him ill. [I'm the same way. Too much rich food and I become ill. Why, I hardly touch lab rats anymore.]

[Do you realize that if this disease spreads, we could lose our entire vampire population? There will be huge gaps in our TV schedules, and when you go to the movie theater to catch a vamp flick, you'll have to stare at an empty screen for two hours!]

Voucher is about to put the bite on Tracer Wetly. Now Knack Night has the bug. Uh oh, he's giving Nuttily that lean and hungry look.

Voucher says to his good friend Wetly, "You smell like Fruit Loops." He puts her in a bowl and pours milk over her. With a wrench, he pulls himself away. "What am I doing? I can't eat cereal with a wrench, " he says.

THE END FOR NOW

THE INLAND (The Island)

The dream police are real! Talk about 1984, this guy has a bad dream and is ordered to report to Tranquility Base at 0800. They have a frequent "lottery," the winner of which goes to "The Inland," a purported paradise. Meanwhile, they are controlled and closely monitored in a huge concrete bunker.

Our hero, Lincoln Logs, questions his way of life. His friend, Jordache 2D, and he, find out they're in the matrix. They're clones and when they "win the lottery" they are harvested for medical use. Sounds dull but they escape into a weird futuristic place. Then out into the desert. Luckily they're kept in good shape because they run for miles. If those two get back to civilization, all heck will break loose. They are supposed to be kept as mindless vegetables according to the law. So the evil ones hire private security to hunt them down.

They find a biker bar. They say, "Hello, I'm Lincoln Logs and this is Jordache 2D."
"She looks 3D to me."
Though they look like adults, the guy is three years old, the girl is four. [Got to love them older women.] This tech guy from the bunker helps them get to Yucca Flats. [Such a poetic name, Yucca Flats. Bound to be a paradise on Earth, right?] They take the maglev to L.A. At the train station they say, "Look, kids! They're so small!" And the nice guy is shot for helping them. They run, just pausing to nail an assassin to the wall.

Then Jordache sees a lady with her face doing commercials. [I mean a lady, with the same face as Jordache, in commercials. Still, not nearly as confusing as time travel stories.] They use the credit card the dead guy gave them. The police pick them up for murder. Better them than the assassins. Who put a tracer on the cop car. Then run over it with a truck.

So our two young clones are on foot, running from a division of heavily armed killers. They hop a freight. That is on the back of a truck. Oh, it's just the wheels. They cut the wheels loose to impede pursuit. There are these huge metal wheels connected by a solid axle. [It's the Dumbbells of the Gods, by Erich von Däniken!] The wheels whack the cars. One big armored truck does a front forward flip. Wild stuff. Couple of jet bikes zoom in. Mr. Clone clotheslines them. Clones borrow a jet bike. It's like a teeny tiny jet plane. How do you put on the brakes? Go through a building, windows and all. They hang on to a giant letter way up on the building. It falls. Our heroes brush themselves off and walk away. They're built clone tough.

Now they say the clone learns from its original. But how? Our two find Lincoln's human guy. He pretends to be nice but nips off to call the bad guys. They get in Lincoln's car. A Caddy. [Now tell the truth, if your name was Lincoln, wouldn't you drive a Lincoln? Maybe his first name is Cadillac.]

So the bad guys finally catch up with them. But which one is the clone? It's a clonal standoff. They're practically identical. The clone has already learned to speak with a Scottish accent. They see the special clone bracelet and shoot that guy. "Lincoln" goes back home. Says to Jordache, "It's me. I tricked them." They kiss. [So, I guess it's him. I don't know, he looks just like that other guy.]

Back in the bunker, they plan to get rid of all the defectives. So they all win the lottery. Lincoln says, "I've got to go back and free the slaves."
She says, "Who do you think you are, Lincoln, Lincoln?"

They nab Jordache. [Where is this going?] She outs with a gun. [They grow up so fast.] They hook up. Put on lab coats so no one will recognize them.

Now the security guy outs with his family history. Here we go. He has clone sympathy. [This thing is pushing two hours. Is this directed by that crazy Peter Jackson? You know, <u>LOTR</u>, the remake of <u>King Kong</u>? No.] Then the bad guy goes after Lincoln with a spear fishing gun.

Turbine breaks, sun pours in, clones run free. They form Clone Town. "Come see cheap copies of famous people. Ride the giant turbine ride." And they all live clone free ever after.

THE END

DESPONDENT HOUSEFLIES (Desperate Housewives)

The girls try to find out the Tin Man's past, but since he grew up in the Outer zone, he has no answers.

Paella is pregnant. It's a miracle, since Raoul's vasectomy. Which he forgot to get.

Snoozin' has second thoughts about finalizing the divorce. She picks up a casual house painter. [Or is this a flashback? Flash forward to the present.] He wants to be uncasual now.

Git Tarzan, AKA Pops Pizza, gets the shock of his life. So he buys a classic car. [These folks need to put the word FLASHBACK on the screen. I don't know if I'm coming or going here.]

Pops Pizza gets a "futon" for his new rehearsal space found by the very attractive real estate or, or realtor for short. Turns out the teenage son is boffing Real Tor. Dad finds out but thinks it's some high school girl. Moms Pizza thinks her hubby is the boffer. He comes home and she says, "I know all about it." Naturally the proud father says things like, 'Boys will be boys,' and 'It's not that big a deal.' Moms is flabbergasted.

[Hey, it says guest starring Lily Tomlin. What is she now, 150? She plays the feisty sister of Mrs. Clutches. They're going to put the Tin Man in his place – a balloon heading for Oz.]

Paella and Raoul have become the pets of a rich lady. At least they already know how to act rich. [Maybe you can purchase people. I thought that was frowned on.] Paella tries to kick at the mule but it's uphill work.

Another twist, Snoozin' and her house painter start over. No sex till the 4th date, she says. But he's actually an artist. He finds that sexual frustration pushes him to be creative in his work. Which he hasn't done for a long time. Snoozin' gets ready but he puts her off, "Just for a few months. Time to work up enough canvasses for a gallery showing."

Snoozin's college age daughter brings home a boyfriend. Well, a man friend. He's at least 40. [Hey, it's Jonathan Harker from 'Dracula: Dead and Loving It.'] Says he's been married three times, "But this time it's serious." Later, at the Fight of the Musical Groups, the elderly gentleman, Jon Harker, hands the bartender a disc. Snoozin' says, "What's that?"
"He's gonna propose during the special song."
So Snoozin' goes dancing over to her daughter and the distinguished veteran actor, babbling about the good old days. To make sure, she "accidentally" super glues herself to the May/December couple. Then Julienne says, "I'm not getting married. Now or ever."

Dare Weems, AKA Tin Man, says to his criminally insane psychiatrist, "Okay, you can meet "him.""" Well, maybe God, because Tin Man kills him. He marinates the body in strong booze for immolation. [Does immolation mean burning? Why not just say that?] Because of a contretemps, they lock the exit door. So Tin Man is going to murder the whole town? [What is the saying for a fire? 'Be small, crawl, don't fall, ass haul?' That's if the building is on fire. If you are on fire personally, you might want to change your lifestyle. The safety saying is, 'Stop! Drop that roll!' No, that's for dieting. Um, 'Shop, rock and roll!' No, 'Schnapps, rot and mold.' No. I'll get it. Check back here later.]

Uh oh, Raoul might get his sight back. Paella has to get herself back in shape quick!

Whoreson gets a bonk on the nose during the big fire. Now he snores. Breed broods about this. So he ends up giving her a double dose of sleep aids, irregardless of her early morning cooking flapjacks and signing books at the mother/daughter thing.

Tin Man goes to the cops, "The boy did it. Pewter Pizza." So I guess Pops Pizza is the one he's trying to get revenge on. [Probably said, "'Tin Man' is the worst adaptation of 'The Wizard of Oz' ever. Especially that Tin Man character."] [Don't get me wrong, I like 'Tin Man,' the miniseries. I'll write about it as soon as I find my copy.]

THE END FOR NOW

ALL KNIGHT RIDER (Forever Knight)

It's the 'French Connection.' A dark lady kills Mario. [Luigi was unavailable for comment.] [In other words, Black Jeans is back. She gets my vote as the hottest vampire babe ever.]

Quoi? She's got a kid. Shirley vampires can't have kids? Then someone shoots at her from a car into her car. She drops in on Nickel La, as she calls Knuckle Night. She says, "Help me or arrest me. I'm not picky."
"Why did you leave me here all alone?"
"Your constant whining about wanting to be human. Got on my last nerve."

Turns out Mario was an arsonist. [Maybe he was the one set that fire on 'Desperate Housewives.'] Jeans adopted his boy. She calls herself Jeans Bonbon and the Knight Rider calls himself Nickel La Bonbon. Coincidence?

She falls in love with a fireman. She finally confesses that she's a vampire. He says, "Is that so? Well, I'm an arsonist, so there!"

SAY WHAT!?! Jeans and Nickel get shot at. She says, "I forgot to tell you, I'M MORTAL.[!!!]" [What Nicholas Nickleby has been trying to accomplish throughout the whole series! And she just mentions it casually like saying she bought some shoes or something! 'I bought some shoes for my MORTAL FEET! NO LONGER THE FEET OF A VAMPIRE! Still smelly though. Vampire or human, feet still stink.]

THE END

DISCOMBOBULATE HOUSEWARES (Desperate Housewives)

Chapter 1 – It's Cliffhanger Time

Uh oh, Tin Man and Snoozin' get to talking. She says, "Actually I was driving that fateful night." So is she going to have a "hunting accident?" Like Tinny tried to arrange for Mook Dolphin? He drew a bead on the guy when, BRING! his cell phone rang, messing up his shot. [Yet another senseless cell phone related accident. An innocent tree was shot. Remember folks, when you go out murdering, SET TO VIBRATE!]

Poop the question. Not a typo. The Great maneuvers Mook's kid into bringing up marriage. Mook says to her, "I've been down that road. It's a one way street. It's a no go. No flip flops, just say no–" she has left the building. Then Pillock asks Snoozin' to marry him. She runs to the bathroom, locks herself in, weeps and says, "I love you and I so needed to hear that. But I want to be the strong single female. But maybe that's wrong for me." Pause, "Are you still there?"
"So I won't be deported back to Canada." [I thought he looked foreign.] She chases him out of the house with a toilet plunger.

The Pizzas hear about this 'make love once a day for 30 days' technique to revitalize a marriage. Only problem is, she's working long hours at her new job. Result? She falls asleep during foreplay. Next morning he's very upset. [I'm not telling it well, it's hilarious. It pays to have good actors.]

So Tin Man invites Snoozin's and son to go hiking. Will there be another timely phone call and protective tree? She decides to marry Mr. Canada so cancels the hunting accident trip.

Miss Patty from the 'Gilmore Girls' palms off a relative on Paella and Raoul.

The cops finally get on to Tin Man but he's taking off for the lake with Snoozin' and PJ's, her son. [Where's Rat Man with his Rat Boat when you need him?]

Chapter 2 – Best Laid Plans

Crazy Tin Man taped a confession so they'd know why he did what he did. Marked it 'Band' and gave it to Mook. "Don't play it until after the murder."
"Okay. Hey, what murder?" But Tin Man was gone. Mook shrugs.
Later Mrs. Mook to be says, "We'll need a tape to tape the wedding."
"Just grab one out of that drawer." [Three guesses which one she grabs. No, the 'Band' confession tape.]

Mr. Breed Bandicoot finds the stolen merchandise and blackmails her. Worse, he puts chives in her Parisian salad!

Cancer Mom feels ill. Dad goes back to college to study china. Majors in setting a nice table. Says to his son, "Hey, maybe we can share a dorm room!"

The sleazy lawyer, Snoozin's ex, hires a guy to rough up Mr. Bandicoot.

Cancer Mom's doctor comes in, "The tests picked up something. You're pregnant."
"What?!? I think I'd prefer cancer."

In the airport, Mook calls Snoozin', "Remember to wash your stinky feet." The Great reaches into her bag for cash to get coffee. She accidentally hits the play button on the camera. A tinny voice comes out babbling about car crashes and revenge. Mook runs out. He calls Snoozin,' "There's something important I have to tell you. Don't freak out. The man you're with is not who he says he is. He has a secret identity. The man you are with is actually Superman! [Oops, wrong show. Did you know Teri Hatcher also played Lois Lane in 'Lois & Clark: The New Adventures of Superman?'] But back to our show. Snoozin' says, "Gee willikers, your flight was delayed? What a bummer. I'll catch you a fish this big." She holds out her hands, dropping the phone out the car window. She says, "Darn, now I'll never know who you really are." They stop to answer a call of nature, then Tin gets a call of police, "We know everything. Put your hands where we can see them."
"You can't arrest me over the phone."
"There's an app for that."
Snoozin' whacks his head with a rock. He's down but not out. They run. He ties Mom by the road, going to make Mook kill the kid with his car while she watches. Sees a vision of his kid, puts the boy out, gets hit himself. Dies.

Chapter 3 – One Dead Dog Away From A Country Song

Snoozin' and Mook are getting married again. He was just about to run off to Vegas with The Great.

The new niece tries to smuggle a hot top to school. Paella is too smart for her. [Or pulled the same stunts as a teen herself.] Raoul makes excuses for her, "She had a hard life, mom's in jail, dad walked out."
"Yeah, she's one dead dog away from a country song."

[Hold on, it's a flash forward. Might as well watch a confusing science fiction time travel story.]

Some new folks buy the suicide lady's house. They have a troubled son. What a surprise. [They should have somebody like the Osmond Family move in, just for contrast.]

First, Snoozin's wedding gown is delivered to The Great, who puts it on. Just the thing to wear while whipping up a batch of spaghetti sauce.

Quotes: "I know I'm wearing men's clothes but I'm not an idiot."

   – Moms Pizza

Paella, upon attempting to bribe her daughter's way into Catholic school, "But you're okay with taking money when it comes in one of those wicker baskets."

The Great, after losing Mook to Snoozin,' "Where am I going to find another man who will make love to me five times in one day like he did?" Now Snoozin' is determined to equal that record. Of course men age as time goes by.

Paella tucks a large check into Father Damien's pocket. "But there are no openings for a new student."
She walks out. After picking the Father's pocket.
'A useful skill will serve you for a lifetime.'
   –Fagin.

Breed and Sleazy sittin' in a tree, K I S S I N G. Or in her bedroom. Whoreson comes home. New friend, Scampi, calls Breed. Is there enough time? [Looks like a job for Rat Man! Okay, Scampi. Maybe she's Rat Girl?]

Mr. Scampi dials on a burner phone, "I'm coming in. But she gets a pass. Black Hawk down. Ten four. Roger, over and out. Ta ta for now. See ya later, Alligator." Then, out of habit, he strangles another young lady. Next, he takes up littering.

Big mistake. All the neighbor women take a self defense class together. They attack each other for real during the simulated attacks portion of the class.

Chapter 4 – When Pigs Fly

Man and wife argue in a small plane. He has a heart attack. Right over Hysteria Lane. [That place is bad luck way up in the air and for miles around.]

It's Xmas in Hollywood. Plastic candy canes, tinsel trees, bickering neighbors, all in the warm sunshine. Ambulance comes, "Holy crap, who's dead now?"
Well, there's The Great, stabbed herself and claims Mook did it. The new kid tried to off himself. In the hospital he says his name is Biff, not Anthony. The nurse "figures out" they're in witness protection. They play along. Later Biff Anthony confesses to her, thinking she knows about his mom being a terrorist.

The Great is the new front runner for the craziest B word on Hysteria Lane. It's a stiff competition.

To get rid of Whoreson, Breed hires his cellmate, Blood, to pose for pictures with Whoreson, a parole violation.

The Great's daughter, Bob Dylan, parents were huge fans, gets crazy Mom to confess. She runs out screaming in her hospital gown and is arrested for flashing the whole town. Oh, and for being totally bonkers and trying to pin an attack on someone else.

The only question is, who is the crashing plane going to land on? The Xmas caroling degenerates into a cat fight.

The dispatcher is telling the lady in the plane, "Look for a large Christmas party to crash into. That will be the most dramatic. You'll get to be on TV!"

Then Sleazy tells Doc about the plane. It has a banner saying, "Marry me Breed, love Sleazy." The dentist decides to rearrange

Sleazy's teeth. For free. They engage in fisticuffs in the Elf House.
PLANE CRASH CLIFFHANGER!

Chapter 5 – Okay, So Who Was Killed Exactly?

Moms Pizza grabbed little Parole, Paella and Raoul combined their
names to make hers, out of the way of the speeding plane. [I knew
it, one or more of her twins will be lost. The new twins, not the old
ones.]

Snoozin' has a fantasy, "What if I never left Sleazy?' She 'swallows
her rage' at him by eating herself into a frenzy. Mook comes in to fix
the plumbing. She tries to seduce him. He runs for the hills.

Sleazy dies. Now it's Breed's turn for fantasy. Sleazy cheats on her.
Whoreson dies alone. All he has is pictures of her. Back to reality,
Whoreson is paralyzed.

Welcome to the Judy Garland School of Acting. Paella tells her
daughter her father fell so she will act sad for a commercial. No
response. "And he fell on your pet." Kid cries. [They told Judy
Garland her dog died to get her to cry during 'The Wizard of Oz.']

Moms's kid is on crutches. So she shaves her head and starts
cooking meth. Calls herself, 'Heidelberg.'

Chapter 6 – And Sleazy Was His Name Oh

It seems Dead Sleazy left Snoozin' part ownership of the 'Live Nudes
Live Club and Bait Shop.' She finds out that Mook Plumber does the
plumbing at the strip club. And sometimes takes in a show. To get
even, she gets a job as a dancer there. She starts stripping for the
crowd. He says, "Okay, I get it." And carries her off.

Crazy Lady says she started fantasizing and went crazy. If that was
the way, every teenaged boy would be certifiable. Let me rephrase
that. [Hey, it's Seinfeld's virgin! She's the local therapist. All that
virginity drove her to become a crazy doctor.]

Paella and Snoozin' are called to the principal's office. They started
a zoo riot. The kids are classified as different animals according to
their "level." Either porcupines, ocelots, wallabies, or fruit bats. It's
obvious which is which.

The girls go to see Catherine the Great. "Come back to the five and dime, Jimmy Dean," they say. Since she has saned up, she understands this.

Snoozin' talks Cotton Candy into quitting stripping. So now she shows up at Snoozin's house, "What next?"

The virgin is in a play. She sucks out loud. Moms says, "I've lost confidence in you as a therapist because of that."
Hubby finally gets honest and agrees.
[She was bad, but the best worst acting award still goes to Xander, Buffy, and Willow for the dramatic reading at the end of the episode, 'The Puppet Show.'] [Speak of some devils, it's Darla of 'Angel' and 'Buffy,' Julie Benz. I had to watch some episodes online and didn't recognize her on the tiny screen.] She advises Breed to give hubby a lap dance. She gets her earring caught, he runs over her bare foot. [See, it's not so easy after all.]

Okay, Crazy Cathy and Dancer Darla decide to take a walk on the wild side.

The Pizza's try to pick out a name for their latest accident. They're batting zero so far. Parker, great name for a valet. Porter, a luggage handler. Penny, the most worthless coin of all. And Preston, good name for a gay guy. [Surely there are professional name consultants? Like for example, not Shirley. Too many 'Airplane' jokes.]

Paella says, "I'm donating an egg so that gay couple can have the same joy we occasionally have with our children." Meanwhile, Lee Press On Pizza isn't gay after all but brings home a mail order Russian bride. [How many stamps go on a package like that?]

She's dead. Eke! [The spell check doesn't like eek.] Mary Ellen finds Eddy, the Monster, left without a sitter. [This is a flashback way back to before the show even started. Is that allowed?]

How's this for a cliffhanger? Pregnant Moms Pizza says to Eddy the Monster, "Hey, it was you killed all those women."
He locks the door. Her water breaks. "Now look kid, I know you're a budding serial killer, but could you take a break from that?" [Do serial killers make good midwives?] Eddy shrugs, "Whatever." The kid is choked by the umbilical cord. Killer says, "What a delicious bit bit of irony, I strangle girls, and now this?"
Moms says, "Stop, drop, and roll."

"Oh all right. I suppose I can unstrangle one for a change. But just this once."

[I guessed it. Elderly nurse dies, but not before she confesses to switching newborns at the hospital. "I'd get so bored on those long night shifts," she said to the priest, "So I would go around switching toe tags on the little ones."
The priest gasps, "I'm aghast!"
"Enough with the tongue twisters, Padre. I repented and put the tags back. Only I wasn't sure which went where. But what the heck, they all look alike at that age. Especially after I had a few drinks."

Snoozin' and Mook move to a small apartment and rent the house to "some guy." [Knowing this show, he'll be a long lost relative who murdered one of the relatives of someone on Hysteria Lane. Or worse.] Yep, it's the one his wife killed that lady and took her kid then killed herself and the guy killed a neighbor lady for being nosy. And the kid grew up to be crazy and then became a billionaire but he was still a loser geek. You remember.

Chapter 7 – Back to Back Flashbacks

The narrator gets a note, "I know what you did last Friday the 13th during the summer Part II.'

Pull Dung is his name. The old killer who came back. All the neighbor ladies run around warning each other. Then he's playing the injured innocent. He killed the first one, her sister tried to frame him but was caught.

Moms Pizza's old chum, Vanessa Williams, drops in. She's like Paella, only ruder. They trade zingers, as usual, but suddenly Moms gets all mad. Then Vanessa says her rich hubby is leaving her.

[Hey, it's Derek Reese from 'Terminator: The Sarah Connor Chronicles.' He plays that rarest of creatures, a straight interior decorator.] He says to Breed Bandicoot, "How about something bold, a bright scarlet red for this room?"
She says, "Maybe a deep beige." [To her, that is bold.]

Chapter 8 – Naughty Snoozin'

Snoozin' takes a part time job doing light housework. In lingerie. In front of a web cam.

Speaking of lust, as Breed ogles her decorator, she backs out the driveway, right into that girl that lives with Paella and Raoul. [I say 'that girl' because she's the one that was switched at birth. No telling who she really is, maybe a Fiji Islander. But what's the big deal? I mean, if you saw some kid running around, eating out of bowls on back porches, wouldn't you put a collar on it and call it yours? I mean if you had the money and the creature didn't have rabies or distemper?]

That creepy guy goes to the hospital. "Let us prey," he says.

[Hey, it's Nancy Travis, AKA the butcher in 'So I Married An Axe Murderer.' And she's a doctor in this. So maybe she's a butcher again.] Breed can't breed anymore so she's seeing the menopause Doc.

Our poor little soft pore corn star, Snoozin', got a call that Rhine and Moms are starting a decorating business, "Sure, I'll do it." Turns out they want her for a nanny. [That's porn prejudice! Oh wait, they don't know about it yet.]

Young Derrick moves in with Breed. Then who comes rolling in but Whoreson Sludge. And he's just as welcome as 200 pounds of sludge.

[It's Major Nelson! And he's a racist. He needs a genie to turn him into a nice guy.]

Chapter 9 – You Don't Have To Be Old To Go Crazy

Paella carries Princess Valley around with her. Not an actual princess, a doll about 18 inches tall. She gets help.

THE END FOR NOW

TOTO (Tin Man)

Zooey Deschanel stars as BJ, a very popular waitress at the Ruby Slipper in Flatland, Kansas. She rides a hog and ditches the fuzz. All very ordinary. But she dreams of a very different place. She has itchy feet and a wandering eye. The rockin' pneumonia and the boogie woogie flu. And the eye of an artist. [Not the wandering eye, the other one.]

Meanwhile, The Sorceress, or Aspidistra, as the Wicked Witch calls herself, consults her cowardly lion like man. He says, "I see a light from the other side."
Aspidistra says, "Summon a travel storm. Take a small troupe of men. And extinguish that light." [The "light" is BJ.]

The bad guys attack under cover of a twister. BJ's parents take her up to the highest window and throw her out. "It's for your own good," they say.
"Yeah, that's what you said to Toto when you cut off his–" and she is swept away by the storm.

She wakes up alone in the woods. Again. There are two suns in the sky. Some small, feathered men drop out of the trees. "Boy have I got the munchkins," moans BJ. [That homegrown will mess you up.]

The head of the troupe reports their failure to Aspidistra. She sucks the life right out of him.

The tree house guys have BJ in a non gilded cage. Along with a guy with a zipper on top of his head. [He likes to change his mind quite often, thus the zipper. Alan Cumming plays the Scarecrow character, who is called Glitch in this version.] BJ tries to politely give a hint to Zilch that his head zipper is open. But people who have had their brains removed are often hard of hinting. The bad guys come. Lounge Cats, they are called, because they always carry portable, battery powered, karaoke machines. What they can't carry is a tune. And they sing constantly. Now that's evil.

They escape and see Tim And and his family being harassed by the Lounge Cats. It's a hologram show. The poor things are tied up and forced to listen to 'Moon River' being caterwauled over and over. BJ releases a guy from a diving bell nearby. Suddenly we're in the Old West. Tim And's name is Wyatt Burp and he wears a star. And a cowboy hat. And a six shooter. No horse though.

He reluctantly agrees to lead the outlander and the no brainer through the dreaded paw paw patch. They find a cowardly lion like man who was captured by the paw paws. [On this planet, a paw paw is a huge, robotic killing machine shaped like a large wolf.] They run from the quickly gathering beasts to the edge of a high cliff over a river. "We're going to have to pull a Butch and Sundance," says BJ.
"Huh?"
"Jump."

The "cowardly" lion like man jumps first. As he falls he yells, "It ain't no thang."
The others jump and yell, "Oh sh . . . . ucks."

Back on dry land, the lion guy, Roar, grabs BJ's hand! He says, "You will go on a long journey. You will meet a tall, dark stranger. That will be five dollars. I have a mobile card reader." Then he heals the Star Man who was nipped by a paw paw. What they call a sheriff in those parts because his badge is shaped like a star. Star Man says, "Thanks. What do I owe you?"
"Don't worry. My service will bill you. I only asked BJ for cash because she's one of those low down Earthlings."

They find the Gold Brick Turnpike and head for Turquoise Town. Zilch asks for a rest stop. Wyatt Burp says no. Zilch says, "Come on Tin Man, have a heart."
"Can't. Left it in San Francisco."
They pull off the road by an old 'Eat Here and Get Gas,' sign. The tiny town is called Hick Town.
BJ says, "My father was always talking about growing up in a hick town."
A sign says, 'No Humans Allowed.' [Now that's just humanism.]
And here come the creatures! Oh, they're humanoid robots. They're about to kill the humans when good old Mom and Pop Jail come running out. [BJ stands for Bird Jail. What with the speeding tickets and the moonshine, BJ was a jail bird.] BJ says, "Hey, my human parents!"
Mom Bot sits her down and says, "We are Series 14 A7 Nurture Units. And don't believe the hype about the new 15 series. They just stuck some 14's into a reshaped chassis."

[Here's a theory, if you think your parents are weird, maybe they're just malfunctioning Nurture Units. What you want is a Series 15, much improved over the old 14 model.] BJ says, "I knew it! You guys are so weird. No wonder I never fit in in Flatland."
The weird flying robot says kindly, "Hold out your hand, BJ." She does and he brands her palm. Moral: Never trust a flying robot on a foreign planet.

They pull in to the outskirts Sapphire City where the streets are paved with bricks. But having no current ID cards, they get some carnies to smuggle them in. Old "friends" of the Star Man. They're off to see the Shell Answer Man, who has the answer to everything. Or used to, before he was fired from his cushy TV job. Now he has a sleazy stage show where he does a mind reading act. When he's not too zonked out on pearl drops. [Played with relish by Richard

Dreyfuss.] His bongo girls spray a mist of pearl drops over the crowd while the Answer Man spouts nonsense.
"He took a great gift and whizzed it down his leg," says a disappointed Star Man.
"He's a real whizzer, all right."

But when BJ shows Answer Man her hand brand, he says, "Go north, young woman. Follow your hand. It's like a compass. See, this finger points north–" the Lounge Cats show up and everybody runs. "Look out, they got show tunes!"

They head north to the frozen land of Nadir. They come to an iceberg and BJ starts chopping at it with a hatchet. The others give a look which says, 'For his we came all this way?' But then her magic hand tattoo thing opens a door. It's the royal palace. Like in 'Sleeping Beauty' only she took a hike. Now what?

Aspidistra and her goons show up. "Where's the Emerald Ziti? BJ says, "If I knew, I wouldn't tell you."
They run. Aspidistra unleashes her flying bats. [She has an interesting way of doing this. You've heard the saying, 'When monkeys fly out of my butt?' No? Then you should get out more. Anyway, she has tattoos of monkeys above her ample cleavage. She exposes her tats [That's short for tattoos. Get your mind out of the gutter.] and the monkeys magically form and fly out from her chest to do her behest.]

Part II: Return to Kansas

BJ wakes up back on the farm! It was all a dream! "Such a dream I had. There was a frozen palace. And I met my real mother, the queen. She was cooking some Emerald Ziti for St. Patrick's Day."
Her father says, "Where did she store the Emerald Ziti?"
"It was only a dream, silly."
"Tell me where she hid the Emerald Ziti!"
"If you're going to yell, I'm leaving." Then the illusion blows away. BJ finds herself with her evil sister. [Did I mention Aspidistra was BJ's evil sister? It's the same old story. BJ was Mom's favorite so Aspidistra fed her a poison apple and sold her to a passing band of dwarves. And really, haven't we all done that to a sibling at one time or another?] The robots call Aspidistra, 'daughter,' now.
BJ says, "You're twisted, sister."

BJ is in jail again. Aspidistra puts the soul suck on the Answer Man. Before he's even dead, his ghost appears to BJ saying, "I am your

father, Luke. Ahem, I mean, unlock the locked cabinet and get out
the Emerald Ziti. The key is lost under the sofa cushions."

BJ tries to get out of jail using her hand tattoo. But it needs
batteries or something. So she befriends a rat. "I'll give you lots of
cheese if you'll unlock the cell door."
The rat says, "Actually I prefer bread. Also nuts and seeds. I mean,
where are you going to find cheese in nature? Think about it."
"Okay fine, whatever."

Then Toto comes and chases the rat away. Then he opens the cell
door. BJ says, "I haven't even offered you a bribe yet."
The dog says, "I'm Toto, dumb dumb. Haven't you seen 'The Wizard
of Oz?' What this show is based on?"
She says, "Smart aleck rats and rude mouthed dogs; I wish I was
back in Kansas." She thumps her ruby colored tennis shoes together
three times, but nothing happens.
Toto says, "It's not exactly alike. What would be the point of that?"
The rude dog leads the gang to safety.

Once out in the woods, Toto turns into TOTO, a large man with Elvis
sideburns. [Hey, it's the police captain from 'Forever Knight.']
BJ says, "Look out, it's a weredog!" and shoots him with a silver
bullet. Luckily she's a poor shot.
"Hey, I'm a friend," he says.

As they head for the Emerald Ziti, TOTO drops a dime on the guys.
The "dime" is a recording chip which is later fetched by Aspidistra's
favorite flying monkey, Snuffers. And they're back in the paw paw
patch. This time there's no handy cliff to jump off of. BJ backs into
a tree, knocking down some apples. The trees all throw apples at
the paw paw pack while our gang runs away.

BJ remembers a lake. Star Man says, "We're just north of
Minnesota. There are lakes there."
"And apple trees."
"That narrows it down."
"And there were lions, and tigers, and bears–"
"Oh my, these clues lead nowhere!"

They find a cabin in the woods. Star Man says the magic words,
"The pigeon flies south with the Winnebago."
The man replies, "But the cow catcher catches no cows."
"23 skidoo."
"And the horse you rode in on."

[All this is to throw off any spies that might overhear. The spy will just think they're raving lunatics.]

The guys are in amaze in a maze. BJ runs along to the center but it's a mess. "I'm amazed by this mess in a maze," she says. She finds the spooky cave. A sign over the entrance says, 'Abandon hope all ye who enter here.' We flash back to when BJ and 'The Bear,' as she called her older sister, went into the cave and released the evil witch. Who looks like a female Gollum. The evil witch inhabits Aspidistra's body and she becomes evil. [Either that or she just became a teenager.]

Part III: Oz Underground

In the Forest of Ewing, BJ finds the heart shaped rock of ages. She skips it across the forest floor, which turns into a lake. A hologram pops up saying, "Luke, you must go to Tattooing and pick up the dry cleaning for the rebel forces." BJ smacks the side of the thing and the right message comes on, "BJ, head south to the Underground. Look up a guy called Ah Homo. I'm not kidding. Wipe that smirk off your face, young lady. Find the Spruce Goose, and the Emerald Ziti, and—Hold on, I have to take this."

Later, Aspidistra steps on the flagstone that starts the hologram. "So, south," she says.

Star Man catches TOTO with his paw in the cookie jar. And the cookies are dime discs. Star Man says, "What's the meaning of this. Speak!"
"Woof," says the miserable dog/man. He sits up and begs them to let him stay.
"Sit. Roll over, Rover." TOTO shrinks down to Toto and they leash him and leave.

In the Underground, they are directed to 'The Sneaker.'
"Where can I find Ah Homo," says BJ.
"Have you tried a gay bar?"
"Not a homo, a guy named Ah Homo. I know it's a stupid name. I didn't name the guy."
This scintillating conversation is interrupted by a raid by the Lounge Cats.

The Sneaker kidnaps BJ. He says, "I am your father, Luke."
She says, "Why does everybody call me Luke?"
"Well, you're a bit of a tomboy. Anyway, here's the doohickey you need to find the Spruce Goose."

The other guys are being slaved along by Lounge Cats on horseback. A wagon is overturned in the road. A guy in a big floppy hat says, "Hey, you guys want some water? I got a bucketful here."
The head Lounge Cat kicks the bucket. Then he kicks the bucket when he's ambushed by some suspiciously merry men. "It's Robin Hat," gasps the head Cat.
Star Man says to Robin Hat, "Luke, I am your father."
"I am your son's cousin's roommate."
"Oh."

The Spruce Goose turns out to be a hot air balloon. BJ says to her dad, "Mom always said you were full of hot air. And flighty."
He says, "I was taking 'The Whiz' when my balloon got caught in a twister. Ended up here. I figured, 'Why not marry the queen of the whole place?' Something to pass the time."

BJ has a special compass. Like the one Jack Sparrow had in 'Pirates of the Caribbean.'
"That's CAPTAIN Jack Sparrow!"
Right, like Captain Jack Sparrow had. Except hers leads to the Emerald Ziti. There's an emerald colored patch of forest. With a hidden door. To the royal crypt. The Sneaker and BJ go grave robbing.

BJ steps through a magic door into a black and white Kansas. The original BJ walks up. Hands BJ the Emerald Ziti. "Guard it well. Green pasta should be eaten on St. Patrick's Day."
"We usually just put green food coloring in everything. I tell ya, green oatmeal just ain't right."
"I hear ya."
"Well, I got to get back to the story."
"See you later, alligator."
"After while, crocodile."

BJ goes back to full color. And there's Aspidistra. She grabs the Emerald Ziti. A ghostly voice says, "What did I just tell you? This you call guarding it well?"

Then Aspidistra locks BJ in the vault. She'll never get out of this. The Zone is doomed.

But here comes Toto to save the day. He runs to Sneaker, "Arf arf," he says.
"What is it boy? Timmy fell down the well?"
"Arf arf!"

"The barn is on fire?"
"Arf arf!" Finally Toto remembers he can turn into a man and simply explain things in English.

At the end, BJ has to convince her sister to quit being such an Asp. The other guys are sabotaging the machine. BJ separates her sister from the old witch. Now it's up to Zilch to remember the secret number to turn off the machine. "One! It's the loneliest number!" It works. The Other Zone is saved! And the humans and half dogs and half lions live happily ever after.

THE END

RETURN TO HYSTERIA LANE (Desperate Housewives)

Chapter 1 – I Know I Left That Baby Here Somewhere

The Vanessa Williams character announces, "I want a baby."
Moms says, "Here. I have plenty."
"Seriously."
"Seriously? From the one person who can out shallow Paella? Why don't you start small. Maybe a goldfish."

Mook and Snoozin' head out for a romantic picnic. With the picnic basket on top of the car. When they get there, with their botched order of fast food, a grackle heckles them.

Back in town, the townsfolk get together to round up a kidney for Snoozin'. They corral the folks and sic a nurse on them for testing.

Snooze and Mook decide to celebrate their love al fresco, if you get my driftwood. Suddenly, the Battle of Bonkers Hill surrounds them. Mook manages to stop the Civil War single handed. What an upstanding hero. Then the car won't start. They see a grackle cackling in an oak with a distributor cap in his beak.

Reign tries babysitting to get her feet wet in 'this motherhood thing' with Moms's baby. The grateful Moms and Pops Pizza go to a fancy restaurant. They hear a baby crying. "Let's go give them that look that we always got." But their wondering eyes espy, a tiny Reign Dear, with their baby nearby. And some other guy. Even worse, a waitress walks off with the kid. Moms follows her. "What gives?"
"That lady gives me 100 dollars to try to quiet the baby."

"How'd you like to make 200?"
So the waitress goes back to the table. No baby in sight. Reign
says, "Didn't you forget something?"
"Your drinks will be here shortly."
"The baby."
"Oh, I got so busy I handed it off to one of the busboys."
"Which one?"
"I'm not sure. He hangs in the back, giving people plastic bags for
cash. But he often says, 'What I'd really like to sell is a baby. Folks
will pay 10 or 20 thousand for a healthy kid."
Reign rushes to the back, only to run into Moms Pizza holding her
kid. "Maybe I'm not ready for motherhood."

Turns out Breed Bandicoot and that weird wife of that killer guy both
are a match for Snoozin'. Breed tells Crazy, "I'm going to donate the
kidney to my old pal, Snoozin'." To beat her to the punch, Crazy
drives by the hospital, tosses her kidney though the ER door, and
speeds a way. [Well, I was just kidding but she goes into the ER,
talks very oddly to the harried nurse, hands her the kidney adoption
papers, whips out her .38, and shoots herself in the head. I guess
that's one way to do it. She leaves a note saying, 'Ha! I beat you to
it, Breed!']

Chapter 2 – Like Mother Like Son

Little Androgynous not only likes men like his mom, he likes the
booze too much too. He does the AA thing, including making a list of
those harmed and offering to make amends.
Breed says, "I know who's number one on that list – me."
"Not even close. Don't be offended Mom, remember when I ran over
Raoul's mom and killed her?"
"Oh that."
She talks him out of confessing to Raoul. Later, she hears that
they're heading out into the woods on a hunting accident trip. Breed
runs to Paella and tells all.
Paella outs with one of her classic lines, "That's the trouble with
sobriety, it ruins people's lives."

Guess who drops in to see Mr. Murder? Good old "Eight Fingers"
Psycho Lady. Dead sister left her his house in the will. Later, 8
Fingers apologizes, "Let's scatter her ashes together. It's not so
much, she only had the one kidney at the end, you know."
"Sure." [These two have been mortal enemies since before the
show even started.]

Breed and Paella rush into the rustic hunting lodge. Nobody there but Raoul. With blood on his hand and a freshly dug shovel in the corner.
Breed says, "Androgynous didn't mean to kill your mother. It was dark. He was drunk and impatient. She took too long to cross the street. It could have happened to anyone."
Then the dead boy walks in. Then the park ranger. [What is this, the stateroom scene from a Marx Brothers film?] "The old bridge is washed out. You folks are stuck here overnight." Raoul is a tad miffed about his mom's murder.

Pops Pizza gets a new job with a big raise and a private jet. That's the pizza biz. They found that delivering pizzas by car was too slow so they drop them out of the air with tiny parachutes attached. A little GPS and the brains of a smart bomb take them right to your door. Be sure to put your tip in the rocket and send it right off. He plans a big celebration dinner with Moms. But he's called away on a flight. She takes another jet, climbs out the window, parachutes down to his plane, climbs in the window, and serves him lobster. [Oops, my cat turned the channel to a 'Bond' film.]

Psycho Dad and 8 Fingers head into he woods to scatter her daughter and his wife's ashes. Of course they are both heavily armed. But they come back best buds. Ah the healing power of nature. [By my calculations, it would take the power of the entire Amazon basin to heal these two.]

Chapter 3 – Who Is Killing Who?

Crazy Lady was faking sanity. Snoozin' is cooking for Psycho Dad and Crazy is slipping poison into his food when Snoozin' is snoozing.

Raoul tells his daughters a complicated story about their grandmother's death. They decide Breed Bandicoot killed her. They and Paella are staying at Breed's because Raoul is angry with Paella for not telling him bout his mother's death earlier. "I thought she was just taking forever to pick up those groceries."
Paella is flabbergasted to see her daughters being obedient and quiet. They even leave a plate of cupcakes untouched. Earlier Paella had said to Breed, 'They're like bears, you have to hang the food up high.'

That night, the girls awake to see Breed looming over them, holding a pillow. In the smothering young girls position! They run screaming from the room. Lock themselves in the bathroom and call the police. That cute detective comes that was flirting with Breed the other day. He says, "I'm going to have to confiscate all your pillows, Ma'am."

Some petard hoisting going on. Snoozin' begs Crazy Lady to taste the brownies she made for Psycho Dad, "I'm allergic to nuts," she says. [Boy is she living in the wrong neighborhood.]
Crazy says, "Well, there's no reason why I shouldn't, is there?" She tastes one, steps out, and ralphs into her purse.

Psycho Dad eats some brownies and collapses. No doubt Snoozin' will be suspected. She's the type of fiend that goes around doing good deeds.

She visits Psycho in the hospital. The doctor comes in, "Looks like you were poisoned by someone called Losing, or Boozing–"
"Snoozin'!"
"That's it!?"

So Snoozin's in jail. Again. When homicide gets a call they must say, "Is it those psychos on Hysteria Lane again?"

Moms and Pops Pizza go to the big candle dipping festival. [No, I've never heard of it either.]

Uh oh, Detective Gay Divorcee is dating Breed Bandicoot.

Psycho finds 8 Fingers has flown the coop so he sends Snoozin' some brownies in the slammer. Not with poison but with a file in them. She breaks out, "You lousy screws can't hold me! Filthy coppers!" She lams it in a hail of gunfire. [Oh all right, she was released because 8 Fingers fled to avoid questioning. But my version is more exciting.]

Then Psycho Dad takes it on the lam in a hail of bullets. Or, he packs to leave. Psycho Dad is being nice to Snoozin', "I baked you some brownies," he says.

Breed tries to breed with Gay Divorcee. She takes him to a gay bar. Several guys greet him in a very friendly way. He says, "I worked here undercover."
"I'll bet you did."
He manages to convince her, but it's hard.

Paella keeps seeing "Creepy Man" from a scary movie. He's like Freddy Kruger.

Give me a break. After all he's been through, Psycho Dad walks into the house, trips on the door jamb, falls, the door shuts. Crazy Lady ties him up. Snoozin' wanders in. She calls the police. Goes out to look, comes back, Crazy attacks her. Psycho protects Snoozin'. Crazy escapes. Psycho confesses. Crazy fumbles the urn, chokes, car crashes. About time.

Chapter 4 – Yet Another Murder

[I've figured it out. The Hysterical Loners get bored and arrange for a murder every so often.]

Snoozin' moves back to the Lane of Death and goes from house to house saying, "I'm back."
Everybody is too busy with their screwed up lives to even have coffee with her.

Paella and Raoul and the girls kill and bury Paella's attacker. Breed's new beau smells a rat. Snoozin' is uncomfortable with the crime. So she and the girls fight and fall into the pool.

Chapter 5 – I Know What You Did Late Summer

Now Breed gets the exact same card Sue Ellen got at the beginning of the show. You know, 'I know what you did last summer on Friday the 13th during Halloween.' [So, blackmailers get confused too. Heck, you could put a similar note in most any mail box in the suburbs.]

For the ladies, Bend, played by Charles Mesure, joins the Lane. For the gentlemen, Paella hires a pole dancer to try to get Raoul back in the saddle after his latest murder.

Psycho Dad calls Breed from prison and says her new boyfriend, a homicide detective, knows about the note. [This show is getting weird.] Now Raoul and Snoozin' are getting together late at night. No, not for that. They chat about the murder they conspired to conceal. And Mook Dolphin sees her with him.

Teri Hatcher has a nude scene! The art teacher says, "I'll have you paint in the nude. Anything to get to something real." After Snoozin' had a giggling fit when he brought out a male nude model. Next class she shows up wearing only a coat which she drops and walks in the door. Everyone else has clothes on. The teacher says, "This is taking casual Friday to a whole new level." The powers that be put the kibosh on the nude students idea. Snoozin' didn't get the memo. She holds up a sketch of the torso of the male model in front of her.

Chapter 5 – I Ain't Got No Body

Mr. Hot Aussie is planning to construct a shelter for the homeless, or something, right where the girls buried the body. He mentions how the EPA kicked him out of a previous site when five spotted frogs were spotted there. I mean they were already spotted. They're always spotted. So Breed and Paella go swamping to transplant some spotty frogs to Dead Man Woods. In spite of Breed's gunmanship, she and Paella are the least outdoorsy folks imaginable. For instance, Paella has frog fear. They finally nab one and head back. Breed says, "It's so quiet," and lifts the lid. The frog hops out right onto Paella, who is driving. The spotted frog almost makes a couple of humans extinct.

It's Halloween. Raoul is haunted by visions of the man he killed. The girls go to move the rotting corpse in the dark of night. Suddenly a voice rings out, "Halt! Who goes there?" They run. Has the moldering corpse risen from the grave, thirsting for the blood of his killers? Find out next week.

"Do you need to move a body? Try our new Body Barrow! Specially designed to move even the heaviest corpse with ease! Act now and get our Shallow Grave Shovel free with each order! Act now!"

Chapter 6 – A Cast of Thousands

Another new character! Snoozin's hard boiled art teacher, famous artist, Andes Zero, played with relish by Miguel Ferrer. [So many of the actors play with relish the producers had to arrange a relish truck to visit the set daily.]

Oho, the Man from Oz hasn't reported the body to the police yet. He says to Breed, "If I call the police they'll put that tacky yellow tape all around."
"We can't have that." Then Breed Bandicoot tries the strangest tactic of all – telling the truth. But he says no. "I'll just wear my blue blockers, hardly notice the yellow tape then." But he relents and hires Mook to hide the body. The girls inform Snoozin' belatedly. She's angry and paints her first real work of art, a portrait of her and the girls burying the murdered man.

A huge critic comes in to condemn the art. [Well, 5 foot 2, but a huge ego.] The only thing he likes is Snoozin's efforts. Naturally she refuses to display her work. After all, it's practically a graphic novel depicting a real crime that she and her friends perpetrated. But, thinking she's just shy, nude scene notwithstanding, Andes Zero smouches her paintings and hangs them in a public gallery. She tries to pull down the main painting but it is screwed on tight. She grabs a drink off a tray to splash at the painting. The glass is fake. It's art too. "Oh, stupid art," she says. [At least that's better than the usual pretentious posing of most artists.]

Paella and Breed rush over and buy all the paintings. But there's detective Gay Divorcee. He says, "I don't know art, but I know what I like." He's instantly arrested by the cliché police.

Chapter 7 – Breed Boozes

She tries to horn in on some strangers. They run. She ends up begging Big Oz for some "zucchini." Later she's about to off herself. May not be needed, somebody runs over Detective Gay. Who made the mistake of announcing the onset of a formal investigation starting next day. Everyone's already started scrounging for tuxes and ball gowns. [For the formal statement.]

Chapter 8 – Winding Down

Moms Pizza's twins come back home to roost. Snoozin's girl is about to have a baby. She plans to give her up for adoption.

Breed went clubbing until a guy was about to club her. Guess who rolled in to the rescue? Whoreson Sludge! You know the old saying: Ugly name, good heart.

And the father is one of the Pizza twins. Hard to say which one.

It was Sludge! Not the baby father, he put the 'know what you did last summer' note in the box. Then he buddies up with Breed again. Says he has a nice cabin, "Away from prying eyes and wagging tongues and those pesky police." Moral: Never trust a man called Whoreson Sludge. Breed insists Whoreson get that special hat she monogrammed for him. He claims to have lost his keys, "Be a Hon, Dear and run down to the office to get one." What could he be hiding? Lots of telephoto photos of a certain redhead? Yep. He rolls in and starts stuffing stalker stuff into a stuff sack.

But he dropped something. In the trash can is the photo of them carrying the body out to the woods. She puts two and two together and gets 22. She says, "You almost drove me to suicide, you puke!"

As she leaves he yells out, "Hey, you're supposed to be nice to the handicapped!"

Mook gets into it with a loan shark. Why doesn't he turn the guy over to the Hysteria Lane Ladies Liquidation Squad, or HILLS?

Sludge drops a dime on Breed.

Chapter 9 – Another Death On Hysteria Lane

[You'd think they'd have run out of live folks by now.] Mrs. Clutches makes herself a 'suicide pie.' Which is mostly eaten by Breed.

Paella and Raoul's kid, Wan Eater, climbs out on the roof to rescue her new cat. [If you don't know, what a cat can get up on, he can get down from. Think about it, how did the animal get up there? He comes down via the same route.]

Chapter 10 – The Final Disc

Breed is busted. Will she go to prison? Will she spill the beans about the others? She hires Scott Bakula. [Captain of the Enterprise on 'Star Trek: Enterprise.'] He says to her, "If I can't get you off, I'll just have you beamed up to the Enterprise." She and he develop a thing for each other until she sees him getting into a shuttle craft with T'Pol. Later she runs into T'Pol, "What is your connection with Trick?"
"He hires me from time to time."
"At the office? Shouldn't you be on a street corner?"
"Vulcans do not have prostitution. We have pone fire instead."

So we end up with a courtroom Dramamine. Snore. T'Pol uses the mind meld on Breed and gets the story of that fateful night. "Call to the stand, Paella Solstice."
"Do you know this corpse," they ask, holding up the moldering corpse of What's His Name.
"Yes. He was my stepfather's cousin's roommate in clown college."
Breed faints. [She's deathly afraid of clowns.]

At home, Paella says to Raoul, "I'll tell them I did it. I'm not a two time felon like you." He's going in to confess. Everyone goes through a metal detector. He beeps. Paella put a knife in his jacket. Old Mrs. Clutches, dying from cancer, confesses to killing What's His Name.

Snoozin' is moving to Smallville. "Maybe I'll meet a super guy there." Pops Pizza filed for divorce after seeing his wife with another man. But it was a gay man helping her with her dress. They finally get back together. It's like the marriage of pepperoni and, um, some other pepperoni.

Chapter 11 – What's Her Name Returns

Remember that other alpha female? Me neither. But she's back. Vanessa Williams is marrying the Lizard of Oz. Paella is promoted to head of V.I.P. sales. [Funny, that's what I majored in at the trade school.] Paella is now the bread winner so Raoul hires the new gardener. The very pretty young female gardener.

Reign is in her million dollar wedding dress with Snoozin', her pregnant daughter, and Paella, and goes what, her water breaks. Snoozin' steals the limo while the others steal another wedding dress.

Moms Pizza gets a big job offer. She's considering it. But only with Pops Pizza.

Breed gets together with Captain Trick.

The new girl moves in, I just hope we won't be bored here." Snoozin' laughs hysterically for several minutes. Turns out Snoozin' had come into possession of this monkey's paw, "I wish for a good life in the suburbs, not a boring one though."

Somebody dies, somebody is born, somebody gets married. [This is an excellent show folks.]

THE END

www.ingramcontent.com/pod-product-compliance
Lightning Source LLC
Chambersburg PA
CBHW021217020426
42331CB00003B/352